Population
Dispersal

Population Dispersal

A National Imperative

John Oosterbaan

LexingtonBooks
D.C. Heath and Company
Lexington, Massachusetts
Toronto

Library of Congress Cataloging in Publication Data

Oosterbaan, John.
  Population dispersal.

  Includes bibliographical references and index.
  1. United States—Population density. 2. Migration, Internal—United States. I. Title.
HB1965.057   304.8'2'0973   79-9672
ISBN 0-669-03615-3

Published simultaneously in Canada.

Printed in the United States of America.

International Standard Book Number: 0-669-03615-3

Library of Congress Catalog Card Number: 79-9672

Dedicated to my wife, Christina,
and my children, John Paul, Anna, and David

Contents

Contents

List of Figures
and Tables

Preface and Acknowledgments

This book makes a clear break with the established view of ever-expanding metropolitan regions. Only a few years ago, most experts were predicting that the vast majority of our population would live in urban areas. In reality, the economic underpinning of the large city, which caused great growth, is crumbling. The new reality, which will see nonmetropolitan areas grow and metropolitan areas decline, is described in chapter 1. We term the phenomenon *dispersal*.

The popular press, largely urban, has not yet grasped the impact on society that this restructuring will have. It continues to believe that the solution to metropolitan problems can be found within the existing framework. Just as the growth of the great metropolis made urbanism a way of life during the first seventy years of this century, dispersal will create a new life-style for the future. Most sociologists and urban scholars have either overlooked or intentionally avoided the study of population distribution. When I began my research for this book in 1971, the idea of nonmetropolitan growth was merely that: a concept. However, the emerging statistics from the 1970s are giving solid credibility to the thesis. Metropolitan newspapers frequently have articles that state that there is a return to the city wherein new residents are reviving declining neighborhoods. Although this resurgence is important, it involves limited numbers. The mainstream of the population is moving in the opposite direction (see the Census Bureau statistics in chapter 1).

The key to the size and duration of the population turnaround of the 1970s is to identify who is leaving the city and who is staying. Chapter 2 identifies contemporary considerations that will have long-term effects on actual migration. The new migrants generally have a higher income than those they leave behind. They have greater concern for their quality of life-style, which significantly distinguishes them from the migrants to the city, who are more job-oriented.

From my early observations of great metropolitan cities, I questioned the rationale of our residential location. As a college student, my initial reaction to the metropolis was one of utter amazement that millions upon millions of people would make a conscious choice to live in a metropolitan environment. I was struck by the antlike feeling as one proceeds to work on a crowded six-lane highway and the individual's feeling of powerlessness to direct the destiny of the city. My first impression of the city has never left me. As I grew older, I began to appreciate the amenities of the city. However, I still felt that for the bulk of the poor and the middle-income residents, the disamenities outweighed the benefits.

The question of why millions of Americans apparently choose the metropolitan living style caused me to review studies by sociologists, historians, and urban scholars on the origin of cities, the growth of cities, and the characteristics of migrants. The philosophy that appeared to have the most logic was the teaching of Ebenezer Howard, as set forth in his 1898 publication, *Garden Cities of Tomorrow*. This book compares Howard to such other early dispersalists as Frank Lloyd Wright, E.A. Gutkind, and Lewis Mumford. The fact that Howard's theories are gaining more validation and more confirmation as time passes is shown. Howard's plans for new towns are reviewed in detail in chapter 5. His view of the garden city has been badly prostituted. This book carefully points out that the infinite spread of the metropolis into layers and layers of suburbs is not dispersal as Howard described it. His concept, in fact, is the antithesis of the American suburb.

Howard's role as the father of the English new towns is traced in chapter 6. We find that while England and France have had achievements with tax-supported new towns, the government-sponsored new towns in the United States have been unsuccessful. The recent cost analysis by the Department of Housing and Urban Development (HUD) is most illuminating in understanding the magnitude of failure of the 1970s new towns. The contrast with Europe is due in large part to the European tradition of direct government planning, long-term policy commitments, and national control of industrial plant location. Population dispersal and preservation of greenbelts, the central tenets of Ebenezer Howard, continue to have application in the United States. However, we conclude in chapter 6 that the English total government sponsorship of new towns remain inappropriate and unworkable in America.

The policy of dispersal as described in this book endorses the revitalization of the 312 communities between 50,000 and 500,000 population and the 5,000 towns with a population of 2,500 to 5,000. The roots and traditions of these towns, which have taken generations to develop, will provide the support for growth. It is not necessary to start from scratch, as was attempted in the HUD new-town fiasco of the 1970s.

This is an optimistic book. Even though a difficult transition period for large metropolitan areas lies ahead, the implementation of dispersal will benefit the cities in the long run. The distribution of the population will allow a new structure, which will transform the city into a place where people will want to live, not just work. There appears to be a balance similar to laws of nature between growth and decline of metropolitan and nonmetropolitan areas. During the first seventy years of this century, the flood to the metropolis depleted the smaller town, resulting in loss of confidence and dynamism. As the scales tip in favor of nonmetropolitan areas, it is important that we as a nation do not overreact. The fulcrum appears to be the point where the amenities and quality of life in metropolitan and nonmetropolitan areas balance, recognizing and admitting that they provide different environments. This proper balance is a goal that we seek. This nation must honestly confront a new population structure. The delay in the acknowledgment of the new structure by the corporate, political, and academic establishment needlessly wastes billions of dollars every year. A substantial part of health, education, and welfare expenditures is spent on problems that are directly a result of overconcentration. Only when the new reality is grasped by the power structure will permanent improvements in the city be possible. Major social forces are unfolding in the migration reversal to the nonmetropolitan areas, which will provide more benefits than huge outlays of governmental expenditures.

My views are limited by the light of my vision, and my assumptions are based on these limitations. There will be different views on this issue of population distribution; however, there will be little disagreement on the significance of the issue. The principles, as enunciated in this book, can be understood by any person of ordinary experience. No specialized knowledge is necessary to understand, endorse, or criticize the conclusions and predictions on future population growth. It is my hope that this book will be read by citizen and politician alike and that they will come to see the new reality as a hope for the country.

Acknowledgments

I am grateful for the research assistance provided by Lisa Ross and Sue Lessenco. A special note of thanks is due to Susan Block. Many sources from her economics honor thesis, "Selective Residential Migration and Mobility: A Micro-Economics Process and Its Outcome," were used in chapter 2. I would also like to thank Diane Swanson, Beth Bigham, and Sue Boersma for the many hours they spent typing the final manuscript.

Introduction

The rural-to-urban migration of the past century culminated in great metropolitan areas that threaten the nation's quality of life. Quality of life includes the living environment, the character of participatory democracy, and the viability of existing governmental units. The solution to the metropolitan deterioration lies in the realization that the existing metropolitan structure is unsound, and the dispersal of the population is a national imperative.

The industrial revolution and concomitant growth of large urban areas have created a vastly improved standard of living; however, huge clusters of people no longer serve a valid social purpose. The technological and communication advances in the past few decades have made the metropolitan concept obsolete from both the social perspective and the industrial production perspective. The existing city is also psychologically obsolete in the sense that it is a threat to health, security, and personal well-being.

To date, American technology and resultant wealth have mitigated the fact that unworkable and unhealthy metropolitan areas have been created. Attempts at alleviating of the urban problem have included a multitude of governmental programs that treat and attempt to heal the existing structure. Many of these expenditures have been wasted.

The third century of this country will see battle lines drawn on the issue of how much is spent and who will pay for the so-called saving of the cities. "Saving the cities" will be the slogan and banner used to obtain massive subsidies for treating the outmoded existing structure. It will once again be proclaimed that additional governmental assistance is the central need and will be the ultimate cure for the cities. Urban studies and proposals that support the existing structure and seek to provide assistance by treating the symptoms are grasped as foward-looking. These programs are considered progressive and innovative by urban scholars. Job training, new housing, model schools, and free nursery assistance, for example, have all been embraced with great fervor until the results show that a priori reasoning as to the structure is sadly lacking.

By contrast, any suggestions for changing the underlying structure are given short shrift by urban scholars. The urban-study textbooks go to great lengths in identifying the problems; however, unrealistic solutions are offered or some type of substantial change in human nature is demanded as the solution.

The apologists for the gargantuan cities set forth rationalizations to maintain the existing order. The fact is that they are unsound. The urban intellectual, whose livelihood is often based on urbanity, is extremely sensitive to criticism of the existing structure. Any criticism of present urbanity combined with extolment of nonurban concepts is immediately classified as rural idealism and is indicted for failure to come to grips with twentieth-century reality.

There is a reluctance to admit that a structural change is necessary. However, the continued treatment of an unsound structure is wasteful at best and creates false illusions of recovery, which at worst causes further deterioration. The proponents of structural change are often criticized for their lack of understanding. They are accused of being craven of heart when they oppose proposals of additional governmental urban programs. The proponents of structural change are also accused of eradicating all positive elements of the existing structure. In common parlance, they are accused of throwing out the baby with the bathwater, even after they have carefully identified that it is the bathwater they want to eliminate.

The urban intellectual, while viewing technological and communication gains as great achievements, has failed to see how technology and communications have made the present spatial structure obsolete. Nor has the urbanologist come to grips with the trend indicated by recent surveys that an absolute majority of urban residents are dissatisfied and would move from the city if they were able to do so.

The major cities are beginning to make frenzied attempts to obtain new governmental programs and to extend temporary aid programs, such as the Civilian Employment Training Act (CETA). The degree and intensity with which a group seeks governmental assistance and intervention is usually a sign that their institution or industry is out of date, unable to compete effectively in a free society, or defective structurally. Governmental assistance to railroads, the housing industry, and the farming industry has, in the long run, wreaked havoc for its intended beneficiaries.

The rational answer to the urban problem is a national policy of dispersion. What is dispersion? Dispersion is defined as the voluntary distribution of the population so as to provide maximum social welfare and productivity in the most efficient manner at the lowest possible cost. As this proposed structural change is defined and explained, the advantages of dispersal and the popular support it will eventually obtain will be seen. The United States has no official, or even unofficial, policy toward internal migration. The time has come in our history for political leaders to be cognizant of movements of population between urban and rural areas and from region to region.

Before federal and state governments start to subsidize the metropolitan areas and attempt to rebuild the cities within their present structure and environment, which are essentially unsuited for human habitation, there must be a concerted national effort toward providing jobs and living conditions that will draw some of the urban population away from the city. This book describes the forces of reaction and certain myths of urban America. It explains that the implementation of dispersion will not decimate the urban centers. On the contrary, the metropolitan city of the future will retain the positive features of urban culture.

The proposition that we disperse, rather than rebuild cities and treat them as they exist, is controversial; however, all important questions of social policy inevitably involve passion. The policy of dispersal will create conflict with the vested urban interests in the short run. However, harmony will come when the urban interests realize that existing cities will benefit from dispersal.

Social problems are often structural. The person who is born in a ghetto family is a recipient of certain family characteristics, expectations, and educational background. It is the rare exception when he breaks out of the family pattern. For the same reason, a group of families operating within the urban structure and environment will not change radically, even though various attempts are made to cause change, as long as the environment remains the same.

One should also be aware that a dinosaurian effect sets in not only for biological organisms but also for human and industrial organizations when any entity reaches a certain size. It is in vogue among city planners and other visionaries to portend a few megalopolitan regions containing the majority of the American population. It will be a sad day for America if Boswash, Chipitts, and Sansan become a reality.

We have long equated modern technology with positive human gain, but, in fact, technology is neutral and can accomplish good or evil. It may be possible that technology can make a megalopolis work, after a fashion, at a very great cost in human resources and in human tension. But equally, technology now makes possible the accomplishment of a great new adventure: the re-created city. It can also endow the smaller city with competitive equality, greater humanity, and ecological superiority. We must demand these things from technology.

Many metropolitan areas have passed the point of diminishing returns in the growth and concentration of population, causing the cost of public services, transportation, government, and day-to-day living to exceed levels that might prevail under a more efficient distribution of population. As noted historian Lewis Mumford stated: "Nobody can be satisfied with the form of the city today. Neither as a working mechanism, as a social medium, nor as a work of art does the city fulfill the high hopes that modern civilization has called forth—or even meet our reasonable demands."[1]

This book is dedicated to the policy of dispersion. It examines the great urban colossus, its reasons for being, and the myths that surround it. Cosmetic assistance cannot save the city. Dispersion will gain eventual popular support, and vested interests of urbanism will slowly accommodate to the national evolution toward rational dispersion.

**Population
Dispersal**

The New Reality

The new mentality is more important than even the new science and the new technology. — A.N. Whitehead

Societies which perceive functions on the basis of the realities long since overcome by time and change do so at their peril. This chapter presents new facts which will render presently held frames of reference as obsolete and indicate that a structural change of monumental nature is underway. We review the reversal of the rural to urban migration, recent surveys on location preference, the impact of the service and tertiary economy in a technological age, and the confrontation with a shrinking megalopolis.

Rural-to-Urban Reversal

The 1970s have been termed the decade of the great turnaround by demographers.[1] An unexpected migration of significant historical importance is emerging. Recent statistics indicate a reversal of the rural to urban movement of the last 100 years. As this shift occurs, the major new residential growth will be in nonmetropolitan areas. To understand the nature of this event, it is necessary to understand that metropolitan areas as defined by the U.S. Census Bureau are large urban areas with population over 50,000 and their surrounding counties. Nonmetropolitan areas include open-country rural areas, small towns, and small urban areas with less than 50,000 population.[2] In 1974, 27 percent of the American population (57 million) lived in nonmetropolitan areas, while 75 percent (154 million) lived in metropolitan areas.[3]

The great turnaround decade of the 1970s has seen nonmetropolitan areas grow almost twice as fast as metropolitan areas. From 1970 to 1973 the nonmetropolitan areas grew 4.2 percent compared with the 2.9 percent growth in the metropolitan areas.[4]

This is a dramatic divergence from the 1870 to 1970 era which witnessed a rural to metropolitan movement. The traditional rural to urban movement remained strong as late as the 1950s which saw the nonmetropolitan out-migration of 6.7 million and the 1960s which saw the nonmetropolitan out-migration of 2.9 million. To put it in striking terms, the nation's nonmetropolitan counties showed a net out-migration of 300,000 per year during the 1960s; however, during the 1970s, the nonmetropolitan counties were gaining 300,000 each year.[5]

1

Calvin Beale, director of Population Studies, Department of Agriculture, was one of the first to note and disclose both the population and job growth resurgence in nonmetropolitan areas. Beale comments on this reversal:

> We have to go back to the pre-1890 period to find anything like it . . . it is not a back to the farm movement. It is in many cases, a back to the country movement with modern conveniences, good roads and nearby small-scale urban facilities. The result is that since 1970, the total number of people employed in nonmetropolitan counties began rising faster then employment in metropolitan counties. This is a major historic turning point.[6]

The correlative to nonmetropolitan growth is the decline in metropolitan populations. Examination of the past thirty years provides evidence that metropolitan growth rates have had a gradualistic decline which merely culminated in the 1970 reversal. In 1970, 75 percent of all nonmetropolitan counties registered population gains, compared to only 50 percent in the 1960s and 40 percent in the 1950s.[7]

In the late 1960s, population stagnation and actual loss in the central cities became evident. Fifteen of the largest twenty-one cities in the United States incurred a central-city population loss during the 1960s.[8] This continued in the 1970s when the central cities lost 1,404,000 persons per year from 1970 to 1975 through net out-migration.[9] More significant is the observation that the growth rate of the entire metropolitan area (including suburbs) has slowed remarkably in the 1970s. The Census Bureau's current population survey reports that the eight metropolises with populations of 3 million or more absorbed 2.4 million immigrants in the 1960s and gained a total of 7.9 million in the 1960s (nearly one-third of the nation's total gain). But since 1970, in a particularly striking reversal of this trend, these areas have lost 0.7 million migrants and increased by a total of less than 0.6 million.[10] Historic metropolitan growth rates are receding while nonmetropolitan places are experiencing a resurgence in activity.

The metropolitan areas of New York, Chicago, Philadelphia, and Los Angeles have virtually stopped growing and the metropolitan area of Cleveland has actually lost population during the 1970s.[11] The importance of this recent maturation is impressive in light of the fact that large cities exceeded the national growth rate in the 1960s. The impact of this great turnaround migration is even more significant when one considers that the internal rate of growth was an important component of the natural rate of metropolitan growth in the last three decades and that there has been an unprecedented plunge in birthrates in the last ten years. It appears the nation's metropolitan areas are faltering most markedly. Urban centers, particularly the largest ones, have been most severely impacted. They are experiencing substantial losses of people, jobs, and wealth.

Projections of future population and their demographic characteristics are, of course, a high-risk field. Reviewing projections of the past causes one to be cautious before boldly setting forth the nature of the future. For example, in *The Future Wealth of America* Francis Bonynge did projections for U.S. populations from 1852 through the next century. His predictions from 1852 to 1900 were accurate within 2.2 percent of eventual population. His twentieth-century predictions fared less well. For example, he predicted the U.S. population in the year 2000 would be 703 million.[12]

Projections of Urban Population by the National Resources Committee in 1937 stated that the urban population would grow slowly until 1945, when it would amount to 70 million. It would then decline to 68 million by 1960. The authors did hedge their projections by noting that the above is "not a prophecy, only a calculation."[13]

As late as 1974, in a report to Congress, the Domestic Council revised a 1969 projection of 300 million at year 2000 to 264 million. This was based on a lower than expected population in 1975 of 212 million.[14]

In light of the above, we refrain from projecting the extent of population migration to nonmetropolitan areas. We do take issue that this great turn-around is a transient aberration or a nostalgic interlude. We project long-term continued flow to nonmetropolitan areas, fully aware that history often side-steps what appears to be a logical future course.

Our comprehensive review of the underlying attitudes of both the urban and rural public indicates that these attitude changes are too deep to classify this reversal as merely transient. Population movements are part of a pendulum-type shift that tends to stabilize. It appears extremely doubtful that this reversal in population movement is a superficial fad. While the ultimate scale of the phenomenon is impossible to determine, wisdom indicates that we anticipate and prepare for realities that are beginning to become evident.

Locational-Preference Surveys

The most compelling evidence that this is a long-term trend is the Gallup and Harris surveys on living preferences taken during the period 1965 to 1977 which clearly indicate an increasing dissatisfaction with metropolitan living.

In 1966 a Gallup survey asked: "If you could live anywhere in the United States that you wanted to, would you prefer a city, suburban area, small town, or farm?" Although only one-third of the sample lived in small towns, nearly 50 percent expressed a preference for such areas as the ideal place to live. Gallup concluded that better jobs available in the bigger cities had many people involuntarily trapped in places in which they did not prefer to live. In 1971 the Gallup organization conducted an identical survey and found that the percentage of respondents expressing a preference for small towns and farms had grown from 49 percent in 1966 to 56 percent in 1971. Gallup interpreted this as a broadening base of potential support for programs aimed at the revitalization of smaller-scale living environments.[15]

In 1972 a survey by the Commission of Population Growth and the American Future confirmed that an absolute majority of the sample population, both large and small town residents (53 percent), expressed a preference for non-metropolitan small town places of residence.[16]

A 1977 Gallup poll of residents in towns of 50,000 and more found 36 percent would move if they had a chance, compared to only 15 percent of those living in smaller places. Only 16 percent of the central-city residents who wanted to leave their city said they preferred the suburbs: they wanted a complete change of scenery. Those who preferred to move were the younger, better educated, and more affluent, predominant working population. The key factors influencing the desire to leave urban places are high-crime rates, overcrowding, poor housing, unemployment or low pay, pollution, dirt, traffic congestion, racial problems, and poor climate.[17]

These findings have been supported by recent studies. The Zuiches-Fuguitt Wisconsin study found this proportion to be 61 percent,[18] while Edwin Carpenter, in his 1973 Arizona study, reported that 52 percent preferred areas of less than 50,000 population.[19] Gordon DeJong in his 1977 study tells us that 76 percent prefer smaller cities, villages, or countryside locations.[20]

The fact that an absolute majority of the American people live in places that are not their preference portends massive locational shifts. These surveys indicate that if people could follow their inclination, populations of our cities would be drastically cut. Correspondingly, the percentage of people living in towns and villages would increase significantly. The disturbing implication of this data is that many people are living in areas which they do not prefer. The surveys indicate their residential satisfaction is inversely proportional to population size of the city of their existing residence. Admittedly, some of the questions asked are implicitly laden with symbolism and allow for a general attitude rather than a reasoned preference. The answers, however, whether well-reasoned or based on intrinsically undefined urge, deserve review and consideration. The extent and depth of these preferences are shown in tables 1-1, 1-2, and 1-3.

One may question the accuracy of the locational preference surveys by asking, "Why hasn't there been greater flow to nonmetropolitan areas?" This can be answered on two levels. First, until recently the plentiful jobs and opportunities for career betterment were available only in the cities. The notion that Americans have "voted with their feet" by locating in great cities is largely dispelled by the above surveys. Freedom of individual choice in job location is limited. Except for the fortunate few who can make a living in any location, most people must go or stay where jobs are. Workers generally do not decide where jobs are located, employers do. Thus the notion that the American citizen can choose residential location by voting with his feet is illusory.

Second, a threshold level of dissatisfaction must first be reached before a household takes steps to move to a new environment. there are a variety of

Table 1-1
Gallup Poll on Locational Preference, National Sample

Year	City	Suburb	Small Town	Farm	No Opinion
1966	22%	28%	31%	18%	
1968	18	25	29	27	
1970	18	26	31	24	
1972	13	31	32	23	1%

Source: James J. Zuiches, "Residential Preferences and Population Mobility" (Report to Center for the Study of Metropolitan Problems, National Institute of Mental Health, November 1974; processed). The surveys are by the American Institute of Public Opinion (Gallup Poll).
Note: Percents do not equal 100 because of rounding.

Table 1-2
Comparison between Where People Actually Live and Where They Would Prefer to Live

Current residence	Percent
Large urban center or suburb	28
Small- or medium-size city	41
Rural area or small town	32

Preferred residence	Percent
Large urban area or suburb	13
Small- or medium-size city	33
Rural area or small town	53

Source: Sarah Mills Mazie and Steve Rawlings, "Public Attitude toward Population Distribution Issues," in Sara Mills Mazie, ed., *Population Distribution and Policy*, vol. 5, U.S. Commission on Population Growth and the American Future, 1972.

constraints for making a location preference into a location actuality. The basic consideration is information as to where to move, cost of the move, the risk of new employment, and the psychic cost of severing existing social and family ties. Since social bonds take time to build, the longer people live in an area, the more difficult it is for them to fulfill their preference. As Niles Hansen tells us: "With time and aging, many city people prefer the environment of non-metropolitan areas, but they will tend not to move because of heavy financial and psychic investments and home, friends, and local institutions and the shorter remaining life span over which the costs of moving must be recaptured."[21]

Table 1-3
Locational-Preference Survey

	Current Residence			
Preferred Residence	Central City or Suburb (greater than 500,000)	Medium Urban Center (50,000 to 500,000)	Small Town (less than 50,000)	Farm or Country
Central city or suburb	43%	6%	4%	0
Medium urban center	1	18	4	7%
Small town	34	34	50	36
Farm or country	22	42	42	57

Source: Gordon DeJong, "Residential Preferences and Migration," *Demography* 14 (May 1977):169-178. Reprinted with permission.

Refinements in survey techniques have resulted in surveys wherein the surveyor attempts to delineate between rural nostalgia and fantasy for non-metropolitan areas versus the actual number of potential migrants. Edwin Carpenter found that 70 percent of his 1,416 Arizona respondents expressed some interest in living in a small place thirty-minutes distance from a larger- or intermediate-size metropolitan area; however, this proportion dropped to 24 percent when conditioned by a $1,000 lost of income. The same relationship held true for small places sixty-minutes distance: 50 percent preference dropped to 17 percent when conditioned with an income loss.[22]

As surveys have become more sophisticated, there have also been attempts to separate the group that merely has a preference for a different location and the group that represents potential migrants. Lansing and Mueller found that one in five Americans would prefer to migrate. When asked about expectation, only about half or 11 percent indicated that they intended to move. Since annual migration across labor-market boundaries is 5 per 100, actual migration is roughly half of expected and the expected is half of desired.[23]

Impact of New Technology

The social, economic, and technological changes of the past fifty years have tended to decrease the need for population concentration. The controlled-access highway is a major factor in decentralization. This highway system has allowed for rapid transport and easy access to goods, services, and people. Transportation has become increasingly less important as a cost factor in the overall cost of goods. This allows for decentralization of manufacturing in smaller places, away from the large consumer markets. It appears that manufacturing can exist better today in smaller places. Manufacturing no longer requires large cities. Small metropolitan areas of 100,000 or 200,000 have a wide variety of manufacturing facilities; and the supply of labor appears to be no problem.

Improvements in communication and transportation have also made possible dispersal of mass culture so that rural areas are no longer isolated from the mores and media of the metropolitan city. The knowledge and skill of the urban worker as compared to the rural worker has become so narrow as to be nonexistent. With the common use of computers as well as telephone equipment, industry and commerce can now be located virtually anywhere. Technology has provided adequate communication and transportation independent of high-density central locations.

The rise of the service economy is closely tied to technological development. Increased productivity due to automation and division of labor has allowed increased employment in the service sector or nongoods-producing sector. (Figures for employment in services are based on the census concept of nongoods-producing industries.) From 1950 to 1970, the percentage of employees in nonagricultural establishments fell from 34 to only 26 percent, and the service-employment sector increased from 59 to 69 percent. As employment in manufacturing declines, the employment expansions will be necessarily filled by service activities. The fastest growing are the knowledge-class categories. This is seen in the increase of professional and technical workers from 3.9 million in 1930 to 11 million in 1970. It is interesting to note the birth of entirely new occupational positions; for example, in 1950 there was no classification for computer specialist; in 1960 there were 12,000; and in 1970, 285,000.[24] It appears certain that the service-sector employment which is relatively free from locational constraints may eventually employ 75 to 85 percent of the working population. Along with the dominance of the service sector is the decreasing need to be near an energy source. In 1935, 30 percent of the labor force was located close to natural resources. This figure was reduced to 7 percent in 1970.[25]

The northern manufacturing cities were built on productive power, massed population, and industrial technology. These early cities which doubled in population every decade at the turn of the century may have outlived their usefulness. A term often used to describe the end of that era and the birth of the present age is the postindustrial age. The move into this new period will be difficult since the transportation, housing, and social systems which served the flourishing industrial technology for the past 100 years are obsolete in many ways. The deep urban labor pool, replenished by European and Southern migrants, does not correspond to the needs of the new technology. The failure to perceive, or the intentional shielding of the light of reality by some urban scholars, creates a transition problem. The longer this confrontation with reality is avoided, the greater the problem.

America does not have a strong cosmopolitan heritage. Our cities are economic creations; and as jobs, purchasing power, and people exit, many traditional purposes of our cities will disappear.

Rising affluence and the increase in leisure time and early retirement have provided many people with the freedom and resources to leave the economically oriented metropolitan area. What is emerging is a new scale of life and work that transcends the customary divisions between rural, urban, metropolitan, and nonmetropolitan areas. The ancient city and the earlier American cities grew as a tool of the industrial revolution to meet people's material needs. The limits of transportation and communication gave no choice but the creation of large, centralized, urban-industrial complexes. Rural areas were needed only for the supply of raw materials. Those who were left behind in the rural areas yearned for the amenities which were the monopoly of the city. This has changed. A new ruralism is becoming possible with the postindustrial age. In contrast to the city being the desired place, city and suburban residents are reaching for the benefits offered by the life in smaller cities.

The Shrinking Metropolis

The industrial base, a former magnet for the cities, now appears to be the key to shrinkage and stagnation. The metropolitan areas with the highest proportion of the labor force engaged in manufacturing activity have had the lowest growth rate in recent years, and actual stagnation is beginning to set in. The disappearance of manufacturing jobs in and of itself results in absolute loss of population. For example, New York, Pennsylvania, Illinois, New Jersey, and Ohio—the heart of the old manufacturing belt—have lost 846,000 industrial jobs between 1970 and 1977.[26] The Northeast alone lost 13.9 percent of manufacturing jobs between 1960 and 1975.[27] From 1970 to 1974, large metropolitan areas as a whole grew an average of only 0.3 percent annually. Smaller metropolitan areas (in the 1 million to 3 million range) continued to grow at an annual rate of 1.5 percent, and were beginning to be strongly challenged by nonmetropolitan areas whose growth rate averaged 1.3 percent annually.[28] These statistics signal a long-term trend that the United States is experiencing a dramatic shift in population distribution.

Due to this transition in the American economy, the former metropolitan magnetism is waning. The smaller town environment will be where employers will build new plants, to which banks will lend money, to which prospective employees will go. Growth in employment is, of course, the chief indicator of future migrational shifts. Thus employment gains in nonmetropolitan areas are dramatic undercurrents which will affect all American cities and will crystallize in new growth centers.

Urban America has had little experience in shrinkage of population and toleration of the no-growth environment, much as individual Americans have had little experience with lowering their standards of living. The initial confrontation of the no-growth metropolitan area will be traumatic. Until the 1970s, the decline of the megalopolis was limited to the central city. The observation of abandoned buildings, exiting population, and disappearing purchasing power was largely attributed to racial, cultural, and value systems contrary to mainstream America. As the entire metropolitan area stagnates, simple explanations for the central-city decline will be forgotten. Public attention will be directed to areawide metropolitan problems. Characteristics which once underlay suburbanization are now being played out on a new spatial scale, national in scope.

To fully understand the transition from industrial to postindustrial economy and its effect on urban America, it is necessary to examine more closely some underlying processes and problems. It appears that the area which will be most affected by the dispersing population will be the northern metropolitan areas. Five key causal elements have been identified as the underlying rationale for the regional shift.

1. Plants and factories in the older industrial regions in many cases are becoming obsolete, necessitating costly reconstruction or renovation.
2. Industries which originally required a large, centralized labor force have been mechanized to the point where this is no longer necessary.
3. Older metropolitan areas have higher taxes, congestion, and more stringent pollution controls which inhibit industrial growth.
4. The transportation and communications revolutions have made heretofore bypassed areas directly competitive of industrial location. Also the widespread use of air conditioning provides the South with a year-round controlled environment.
5. The growth areas in the South and West tend to be more politically receptive to new industry. The city councils of southern towns generally take the initiative and welcome new industry. The fact that they are growth-oriented makes for a dynamic civic spirit.

As stagnation ensues, various traumatic shocks to the metropolitan structure will become apparent. Per capita income generally follows the direction of the migration. Thus the exited area faces both lower total income and lower per capita income. The metropolitan revenue base suffers as the out-going migrants generally comprise the younger, more educated, and higher-income households.[29]

The future reduction in metropolitan income will require reduction in public services. Any reduction in services is not easy, but it will be especially difficult for largest-size cities since they have the highest per capita rates of public service expenditures. A 1972 survey shows operating outlays of $283 per person in cities over 1 million compared with $95 for cities with less than

50,000 residents.[30] The metropolitan area is thus on the horns of a dilemma: either increase taxes to a poorer citizenry or reduce public services to a citizenry which often requires more services. Raising taxes appears to be the least viable alternative since it will merely increase out-migration.

The ability of city officials to reduce public expenditures is marginal. State and municipal employee unions are the fastest-growing unions in the country, and their power is exhibited by the fact that the public-wage increases have been greater than those of the private sector.[31]

It is undisputed that as a metropolitan area grows, per capita service costs increase. This is not due solely to more comprehensive public services. The largest standard metropolitan statistical areas (SMSAs) spend more for comparable public services than smaller ones.[32] To date, this imbalance has been largely mitigated by the fact that the residents of growing metropolitan areas have had above average income per capita. However, as the largest SMSAs are experiencing net out-migration, their income per capita no longer provides the cushion for higher-cost public expenditures.

There appears to be a direct correlation between high-cost-of-living areas and out-migration. The urban areas with the highest cost of living between 1970 and 1974 experienced new out-migration, while those with the lowest living cost had substantial in-migration, according to recent census data on migration.[33] It is a self-fulfilling prophecy: the out-migration causes higher per capita costs, which in turn creates an additional out-migration. Clearly, this is a vicious cycle.

An added impetus to the metropolitan stagnation is the restraint on property values. The higher tax base and the lessened demand tend to diminish property price levels. For example, the price of the average single-family home increased about twice as fast between 1966 and 1971 in growing cities in comparison to declining ones.[34] In the long run, this process will slowly erode the present metropolitan structure. There will come a time when it will become a crisis, and a basic decision will have to be made. It is a question of higher taxes with eroding population or drastic cutback of city government. Since increased taxes will only accentuate out-migration, the course of the future appears to be a reduction of expenditures. There will be increased pressure to reduce expenditures, an event which is particularly painful, given its fragile private-employment base.

Along with the necessary restructuring of the aging metropolis faced with dim fiscal prospects, there will be an interregional metamorphosis. The thrust behind the shrinkage of the metropolis and the expansion of other areas is due to certain characteristics of the American psyche.

Brian Berry identifies certain poignant elements of the American personality which have fostered the redistribution of the American population, first through suburbanization, but more recently on a larger spatial scale.[35] Americans are characterized by a love of newness, a factor which has proven beneficial to the American economy, but which has often led to a greater emphasis on new construction rather than renovation and preservation of older facilities. The desire to be near nature is a second element of the American character which has led the population to redistribute itself. This has often been linked to the American spirit of frontierism. The strong beliefs in individualism and the freedom to move are two characteristics which may have their source in the American tradition of liberal democracy. From the urban standpoint, this feeling of individualism translates into a strong national preference for the one-family house and a general emphasis on privatism. Another element has been variously termed the melting pot tradition and the land of opportunity. It refers to the fact that upwardly mobile classes in America usually move on to new locations. A final characteristic identified by Berry becomes intermittently visible on the urban landscape; namely, the violence which results from the struggle by the less fortunate who are left behind to enter the mainstream of the nation's economic life.

The combined effect of all these underlying processes is the increased viability of the nonmetropolitan area. When one considers plant location from the executive viewpoint, the growth of the medium-size centers and the relocation of business in the South is more easily understood. This is important since population follows jobs. A business executive charged with the responsibility of increasing profits faces the decision of where to locate new plants. Traditionally, the service facilities of the metropolitan area and its proximity to corporate headquarters determined that the vacant land in the suburbs would be the recipient of new plants. More recently, nonmetropolitan areas and locations in southern and southwestern states have become the favored areas for industrial development. A review of the most basic considerations of plant locations further indicates that dispersal and the interregional shifts are the wave of the future.

A business executive analyzing where to locate a new industrial plant might consider the following factors in comparing a metropolitan to a nonmetropolitan location.

Taxes. Real estate taxes are higher in metropolitan than in nonmetropolitan areas. As a metropolitan area grows, taxes per capita tend to rise. This is due to a larger expenditure for comparable public services than in smaller towns. These services are also provided by entrenched municipal unions which have strong power to establish wage guidelines. The complexity of the police, fire, sanitation, and general administration increases with size, requiring higher per capita taxes.[36]

Building Costs. The cost of new plant facilities is greater in high-intensity areas, principally because of higher land costs, high wages, and completely unionized construction trades. This consideration is easily benchmarked.

Usually a specific dollar amount must be authorized before construction of a new plant. When a company has an initial investment which may be 25 to 30 percent smaller, there must be important overriding reasons to locate in the higher-cost areas.

Wages. The wages in nonmetropolitan areas are generally lower.[37] The traditional low wages are in large part due to the absence of unionization.

Utility Costs. This cost of doing business has taken on new importance in light of the rising cost of energy. As America begins to react to the fact that foreigners control approximately 50 percent of the oil reserves and realizes that the supply of fossil fuels is being rapidly depleted, the cost differential between northern and southern cities becomes increasingly important. On top of this is the fact that three or four months of subfreezing weather in the North requires large amounts of heating fuel.

Cost of Living. Cost of living is higher in the larger metropolitan areas. The Boston and New York regions have the highest cost-of-living statistics in the country. Boston's living cost is 36 percent above that of Austin, Texas.[38] The price for a newly built single-family home in the South is 25 to 30 percent less than in the Northeast.[39] It is interesting to note a correlation between cost of living and size of communities. The larger the city, the higher the cost of living.

Tax Abatements. Competition for industries and jobs has created various tax incentives, low-interest municipal bonding, and tax abatement for a ten-year period. The ability of smaller towns in the southern region to attract industry has sometimes been attributed to these inducements. Metropolitan areas are simply in no position to offer tax abatements when their troubled fiscal systems need every dollar for their operation.

Transportation. The interstate highway has allowed long-haul trucking to become the dominant mode of freight transportation. Thus variability in location is more possible. Transportation costs are becoming smaller as compared to production costs. As this occurs, the smaller decentralized plant becomes feasible.

Conclusion

Many urban experts have failed to grasp the fact that the city has outlived its evolutionary role. The failure to recognize the new reality may be due to a sense of inevitability of the present urban form. Many believe that even though large cities create problems, they are necessary if we are to maintain a high standard of living. This fatalistic view that accepts the metropolis as an inevitable concomitant of advanced industrial society will change. The epoch in which cities become continuously larger and more complicated is rapidly coming to an end.

Technologically, modern people have overcome time and distance. The three main needs which for centuries only cities could fulfill—easy communication, the propensity of goods and people, and power—can now be satisfied outside the urban organism.

Models of reality are useful as long as they are predictive. When permitted to age without adjustment to new facts, they can be positively harmful. There is a danger in emphasizing localized problems when massive shifts on a national plane are occurring. In the past decade, when new migrations were beginning, the media centered on confrontations and internal shifts within the metropolitan areas. Unnoticed was the fact that the older northern industrial cities were losing residents who had chosen to live in dispersed population groupings.

The stream of time flows past and carries the realities of yesterday. The undisputed fact that metropolitan areas have stabilized and are losing population is the harbinger of the new reality. At the end of the nineteenth century the fast-growing metropolis had been credited with the creation of a system of social life founded on entirely new principles. A short half-century later the future of the metropolis is uncertain. A poignant benchmark which reflects a basic transformation is the fact that as many blacks are moving to the South as are moving from the South. The new reality of nonmetropolitan growth is gaining more and more momentum due to a rising consciousness of environment and quality of life. Outdoor recreation available year around, attractive scenery, and shorter workweeks create a fashionable image that is strongly weighted in favor of smaller towns.

We are passing through a revolution that is challenging metropolitan structures. The morale and confidence is passing from the older metropolitan areas to smaller towns and new regions. After an immense literary outpouring on urbanity along with its problems and solutions, the age of the city as the predominant force in our society may be at an end.

2

The Migrants:
Who and Why

To tell them that they cannot help themselves is to fling them into ruthlessness and despair. —J.A. Frude, *Short Studies in Great Subjects*

Characteristics of the New Migrants

The evolving conceptions of city, country, and the good life make the migrants of today much different from those of the 1890-1970 period. The concept of the city—good jobs and excitement compared with the concept of the nonmetropolitan areas as the reservoirs of stagnation—has changed drastically. Today the metropolis is often viewed as frenzied, deteriorating, and polluted. In the pre-World War II movement, opportunity lay in the economic growth of cities; today the younger generation perceives that opportunity lies in clean air and smaller-scale living. The period of rural to urban migration was a time of unencumbered economic growth; the current period is one of resource shortage and environmental deterioration accompanied by relative affluence.

Rural-to-Metropolitan Migrants

The first comprehensive study of migration to the city was Adna Ferrin Weber's masterpiece entitled *The Growth of Cities in the Nineteenth Century*. Weber found that more women migrated than men, but for shorter distances, and for marriage rather than paid employment; that the migrants tended to be young adults, more than half usually in the 20-to-40-year age range; that as much as 80 percent of the adult population of the great cities was of outside birth and that two-thirds of the immigrants had lived in the great cities for less than fifteen years. Weber found that the cities contained a larger proportion of women and foreigners than the rest of the country and had divorce rates three to four times those of the country.[1]

There appears to be little dispute that the pre-1970 metropolitan migrant was younger, more educated, and more productive than those he left behind. Models of migrants indicate the highest rate of mobility occurred during the first few years after marriage. Mobility was greatest in the 18 to 34 age group. College-educated persons had a high tendency to long-distance moves. Persons with a history of moving were likely to move again, and renters were found to be more mobile than home owners.[2]

The overwhelming majority of studies indicate that movement to metropolitan areas was education selective. For all the age-sex groups common between all regional areas, the median educational level of migrants out of rural areas was higher than that of persons who did not migrate. These educational differences were most pronounced in men aged 35 to 54 and held true for both white and nonwhite migrants.[3]

Furthermore, movement to metropolitan areas was usually for economic reasons, most often new employment. A 1946 survey indicated that over 50 percent of the migrants moved to the city to take a job (40.2 percent) or to look for work (11.7 percent). The same survey also found that in the peak age bracket, 25 to 44, economic reasons accounted for two-thirds of all moves.[4] In a 1962 survey, Lansing and Mueller concluded that 58 percent of moves to the city were economically motivated and an additional 14 percent were for partly economic reasons. Thus making allowance for movers where no reason was given, three moves out of four were at least partly economic.[5]

A study by the Bureau of Labor Statistics in 1964 indicated that economic motives were predominant: "Half of migrants reported work-related factors to take a job, look for work, or make a job transfer, as reasons for these moves."[6] This led to the conclusion by Lansing and Mueller that "the decision to move among members of the labor force is strongly dominated by job-related economic reasons."[7] Peter Morrison, in his 1972 survey, found that people migrate primarily in response to economic forces. He concluded that "they tend to be pulled to where the jobs are."[8]

The decline of agricultural employment caused both the employed and unemployed to look to the cities. Some had no choice, while others sought better employment. The image of economic gain and association of higher wages with metropolitan areas was supported by statistics. Traditionally, incomes have been consistently above the U.S. average in standard metropolitan statistical areas (SMSAs) greater than 1 million in population, around the national average in northern SMSAs below 400,000, and about 15 percent below this average in southern SMSAs. Until recently, earnings tended to increase with city size for all workers, white and nonwhite.[9]

Whereas noneconomic considerations play a large role in the migration to nonmetropolitan areas, they played a minor role in the migration to metropolitan areas. In other words, migration from agricultural areas did not occur due to the acquisition of a distaste for farm life. It appears that rural residents would have preferred farm life had the economic opportunities in agriculture stayed approximately equal to those in other sectors of the economy.

Migrants to metropolitan areas are apparently motivated to move from their homes because they are not earning an adequate level of income or cannot find the right sort of employment. That is, rural to urban migrants were career-oriented. The group that gave noneconomic reasons for the move to the metropolitan area was small in number and consisted basically of young workers and the very poor.[10] Young workers moved because they were anxious to reunite with their family or because a family member or friends already lived in a metropolitan area. Movement based solely on family and friends is often an irrational economic choice since young workers may arrive in places where an oversupply of unskilled labor already exists.

Since migrants to the metropolitan areas were economically motivated and career-oriented, they often left behind a disproportion of lower-income, less educated, and less skilled people.

Metropolitan-to-Nonmetropolitan Migrants

The 1970s were coined by one writer as the decade of the great population turnaround in America.[11] The early 1900s through 1960 was characterized by a continuous stream of people from rural and small towns to metropolitan centers. As late as 1950-1960, nonmetropolitan counties in the country experienced a net out-migration of 5.5 million persons.[12]

A dramatic reversal has occurred since 1970. It is estimated that metropolitan areas grew at an average annual percentage change of 1.5 percent and nonmetropolitan areas at 0.7 percent during the 1960s. In 1970-1975, on the other hand, metropolitan areas grew at an average annual percentage change of 0.7 percent and nonmetropolitan areas at 1.2 percent.[13] The current distribution trend is real and substantial and seems likely to continue at least through the next decade.[14]

The new urban to rural migration is unique and distinct in motivation, numbers, and territory. It appears to be smaller in numbers and in scale than the movement to the cities. The overall group appears to have more balance in terms of age and different values, and economics holds a less determinative role. The earlier migrants to the cities were pulled by the economic factors of attraction rather than dissatisfaction with the status quo. The migration of the 1970s away from the cities indicates that dissatisfaction or a push syndrome may play a greater role. Perception of the mounting crisis in the city has become widespread. People are increasingly aware of the problems of dirt, noise, crime, crowding, and energy shortages. Various psychological studies found that the avoidance of metropolitan problems was one of the most widely held motivations for the movement from the city. A Harris survey in 1970 indicated that while 24 percent of the respondents living in metropolitan cities thought their community was not as good as it was five years ago, only 5 percent of the nonmetropolitan residents stated their communities were not better than five years before.[15] This is supported by a 1975 Gallup poll which shows rural residents have a much greater satisfaction with their residential location as compared to urban counterparts.[16]

Although there are differences, there are also similarities. The new move-ment is again based on a perception of opportunity gradients. This opportunity, however, is not dependent on pure economic considerations. Migrations to smaller towns are in some aspects a departure from the materialistic "more is better" philosophy. This is seen in the finding that migration to nonmetro-politan areas is generally to counties with lower income than the metropolitan areas, even though the income differential is narrowing.[17]

The present migration is not in response to a massive shift in labor needs. Climate, life-style, and residential environment are important motivating con-siderations. The relative number of people involved in the migration is smaller and its pace is slower. The essence of growth appears to be in the geographic sense, the redistribution of population within already determined boundaries.

This dispersal trend is more intricate than the 100-year migration to the cities. It is simplistic to label this an urban to rural movement. The fact that space is no longer a barrier creates a new social relationship.

Recent surveys indicate job opportunity and economic advantage do not rate at the top of the preference scale as they did in the rural to metropolitan surveys. Migrants to nonmetropolitan areas most frequently list reasons such as better neighborhoods, schools, or climate. Family considerations such as marriage or divorce are the next most frequent reasons, followed by job opportunities. The particular area qua area is more important than economic opportunity. This is supported by a recent Michigan study which found that migrants to nonmetropolitan areas of Michigan ranked economic opportunity as third, with only 16 percent citing either jobs or business interests as pulling them there.[18] Recent data indicate that the new immigrant families to non-metropolitan areas tend to be young, well educated, and concentrated in profes-sional and managerial occupations. In Maine, for example, as of 1970, 8 percent of adults aged 25 or older had completed four years of college. In sharp contrast, 44 percent of the immigrant household heads had achieved this level of educa-tion.[19] High-education attainment is a social characteristic which has been tradi-tionally associated with the urban middle class rather than with rural life.

The high-education attainment of the immigrants leads them to support improvements in the educational system of their chosen communities. The Maine study also supported the fact that income was not the predominant deter-minative for the move. This study reported that half of the immigrant house-hold incomes were less than before they migrated. It appears that they moved not because of economic necessity but rather to enhance the quality of their living environment.

Interregional Migration

The dynamics of the trend from metropolitan to nonmetropolitan areas is also affected by the significant changes in regional migration. While admittedly much of the interregional migration is from large city to large city, the phenomenon is relevant to population dispersal. The grass-roots reasons for interregional migration are the same for migration to the nonmetropolitan areas. Migration in the 1970s and 1980s is due to dissatisfaction between the place of origin and the place of destination. The residents in the early part of the century traded off disamenities of the city for higher wages. As the wage differential narrows and disamenities grow, this trade-off becomes less attractive. The median family income gap between metropolitan and nonmetropolitan areas has narrowed considerably, and the differential now is only about 20 percent according to Zuiches and Carpenter.[20] In real terms, this income differential shrinks even more if one takes into account that property taxes and cost of living generally are quite a bit lower outside metropolitan areas. Since families have more money over and above bare sustenance needs and greater financial security to venture their life savings on moving expenses and a home in the country, the turnaround may reflect the desire and opportunity of American families to live out their preferences.

Interregional migration is the national counterpart to suburbanization. The aim is often insularity from the deteriorating environment and place of origin. The underlying rational is thus similar to the movement to nonmetropolitan areas. Metropolitan to nonmetropolitan migration is in part due to a momentum which is sweeping employment and population growth away from the older metropolitan centers in the northeastern and northcentral states to the newer growth poles of the South and the West. Local planners cannot act within the immediacy of their domains without being cognizant of these realities. There is a danger in emphasizing localized problems without considering the broader picture of massive shifts on the national scale. In the past decade the media focused on the flight to the suburbs; unnoticed was the more important interregional shift.

People follow jobs, according to many authorities. Therefore it is imperative that we review where the employment has been growing in the United States. In the fifteen-year period between 1960 and 1975, the employment base in the United States has increased by 46 percent. This growth was far from evenly distributed throughout the country. While the Northeast secured only a 21 percent increase and the northcentral region a 36 percent increase, employment in the South and the West expanded by nearly 70 percent. By 1975 the South has become the dominant employment locus of the country.[21] To put it in striking terms, the South has added seven additional jobs for every ten that existed in 1960; and the state of Georgia had an employment growth rate of nine times that of the state of New York between 1967 and 1972.[22]

This monumental change in job growth became evident in 1970-1975. During that five-year period there was an absolute job decline in the Northeast, whereas the South captured more than one-half of all the new economic growth in the United States. While the Northeast has lost over 781,000 manufacturing jobs from 1960 to 1975, the northcentral region experienced only minimal change, but the South increased with enormous vigor, adding almost 1.5 million manufacturing jobs to its employment rolls. In 1960 the Northeast was the dominant manufacturing center of the nation, with the north-central region closely competitive. By 1975, however, the South had surpassed the Northeast and now challenges the stagnant northcentral region.[23]

Studies indicate that economic factors did play a vital role in intermetro-politan migration; local employment opportunities and income characteristics at destination proved to be significantly predictive of a region's relative rate of migration. People head to places that are growing the fastest, which results in a self-fulfilling prophecy. Furthermore, the northeastern and northcentral regions have shown gains in per capita income below the national average, while the South is growing at rates above the national average; this trend accelerated between 1970 and 1976. In contrast, the middle Atlantic, east northcentral, and west northcentral divisions which had below average income gains showed heavy out-migration during 1970-1976.[24]

An additional income incentive for interregional migrants may be the overall cost-of-living differentials between such regions. Recent census data on migration to and from metropolitan areas show that all the high-cost areas experienced net out-migration during 1970-1974, while the low-cost areas had considerable net in-migration.[25] Energy costs and taxes are a major part of the cost of living. Energy costs in metropolitan areas in the Northeast are 97 percent above the national average while those in the sunbelt are signif-icantly below the average.[26] It seems very likely that the lower living costs in the sunbelt will continue in the near future to attract in-migration, espe-cially as the cost of fuel continues to increase. Many of those coming from the northern realm are lured by lower taxes and economic advantages. While migrants from the Northeast may like services, they have no intention of tax-ing or creating governments to achieve them. Since northern migrants are gen-erally better educated and wealthier than those left behind in the North and Northeast, their political outlook must be described as conservative. They often think of their less tolerable northern living experiences as being the re-sult of high taxes and deteriorating environments.

The interregional migrant is often the retiree. Senior citizen migrants are strongly motivated by noneconomic factors such as climate, friends, fam-ily, and easygoing quality of life. The interregional migration subject cannot be treated without placing a high importance on the noneconomic influence of climate. Along with climate, the cost-of-living consideration is crucial since many retirees are on fixed incomes. The elderly will be an increasingly im-portant segment of the population when one considers the higher median age and lower birthrate of the last decade. The South and West have been the overwhelming favorites when it comes to retirement choice. Recent re-ports indicate that between 1970 and 1976, while elderly population nation-wide increased 14.8 percent, the South and West scored gains of 22.1 percent and 20.5 percent, respectively, in persons age 65 and over. By contrast, the elderly population in the northeastern and central regions grew by a smaller percentage than the national average.[27] The interregional stream has been selective of the more well-to-do, better educated, older, more conservative northeastern and northcentral population. However, as more jobs are created in the South and the overall locational preferences continue to mark the South and West as the preferential areas, the overall population will increase most drastically in those areas. The mid-decade survey shows that the nation has gained 10 million in population since 1970 to a national population of 213,121,000. Eighty-five percent of the growth was in the twenty-nine southern and western states. The only northern states to gain more than the national average of 4.8 percent were Maine, New Hampshire, and Vermont, all largely rural.[28]

The classic sociological-psychological question of whether preferences lead to behavior is being answered when it comes to migration. In one of the most fascinating nationwide studies on regional residential preferences, David Morgan was able to determine from his questionnaire the changes in population distribution that would occur if everyone desiring to live elsewhere were to move to their preferred region. He fount that:

> The largest increase, 124 percent, would occur in the mountain states, followed by a 41 percent increase in the Pacific division. The south Atlantic states would show an 11 percent increase, while the west south central would grow by 1.3 percent. The Middle Atlantic, east north central, and west north central would lose 27, 25, and 21 percent, respectively, of their populations if everyone desiring to live elsewhere could move to their region of preference.

Of course, not all the respondents were potential migrants, and perhaps many will never think of actually making a regional move. It is important, however, to note how closely Morgan's results correlate with actual demographic trends.[29]

The majority of our economists and urbanologists have been concerned with whether there has been employment growth in the cities, central cities, or the suburbs. In reality, the job rise and job decline is working itself out over the entire geography of the country, and their parochial inquiry must be broadened.

Conclusion

Many scholars, after examining the qualities of the migrant, see a bright future for nonmetropolitan growth. Migrants from metropolitan areas tend to be slightly older, better educated, and less economically motivated. With these characteristics, as the structure of the population shifts upward in age, social security payments become more comprehensive, and early retirement becomes more prevalent, there will be an increased percentage of the population moving to nonmetropolitan areas.[30]

Former restraints on moving to new areas seem to be losing their grasp. As the educational selective stream continues to leave the congested metropolitan areas, we can expect the less well-to-do and educated to swell this stream. Rising levels of income, opportunity, and accessibility will make earlier constraints less confining.

Finally, the circular dynamics of the process of residential mobility are self-reinforcing. Migration occurs because groups of families become dissatisfied with some aspect of their environment. They move, and in turn influence the economic, physical, social, and political environment of the place they left behind. This causes still more families to become dissatisfied and move, and discourages other families from locating where they potentially may have located. Migration also occurs because groups of families are pulled toward some environmental aspect of an area. The destination of these households will be affected by their arrival; there may be growth and further immigration. Alfred J. Brown tells us that: "Since migration tends to be selective and stagnation or decline often makes for an unattractive environment, net out-migration from a community may have a self-reinforcing quality as may net in-migration for corresponding reasons."[31]

Blackwood and Carpenter, in an exhaustive treatment of residential preferences and migration patterns, conclude that out-migration from cities for a significant proportion of the population is inevitable. They conclude that the force of antiurbanism is such that efforts to reverse or halt out-migration from metropolitan areas by making cities more attractive may be hopeless, especially in light of the changes which seem to be facilitating the ease of migration to nonmetropolitan areas.[32]

3

Dispersal and Why

He that will not apply new remedies must expect new evils: for time is the greatest innovator.—Sir Francis Bacon

This chapter views the failure of the human cluster in the form of conurbations, the myths of urbanity, the futility of the pleasure-garden path, and the fact that cosmetics will not work.

The population will eventually be stabilized in a more balanced distribution, with medium-size cities serving as the growth centers for the future. Dispersal of population will continue to occur. This reversal of the rural to urban migration will contribute to the life, liberty, and pursuit of happiness of the citizenry.

Dispersal is defined as the voluntary distribution of the population so as to provide maximum social welfare in the most efficient manner at the lowest possible governmental cost.

Clustering Is Obsolete

We have seen the momentum of the cluster concept over the past 300 years. From orderly medieval villages, human settlements have grown to 9 million and 10 million population conurbations. Once energy was harnessed, first by discovery of coal and then by oil, the industrial revolution began its munificent production. Concentration of wealth began to benefit the cluster areas. Capital was invested over and over until huge economies of scale became the byword of the twentieth-century industrial revolution.

Some opine that there is an inexorable march to the metropolis and that any attempt to halt or to control it will fail. Jane Jacobs, for example, considers large conglomerations of human beings the natural habitat of mankind. She considers the city to be a form of nature as are colonies of prairie dogs or beds of oysters.[1] Her message is to accept the metropolis and its unsurpassed productivity and to spend energy on making the metropolis better.

Jacobs asserts that metropolitan defects are due to a lack of concern by the citizenry; and if money, taxpayers' of course, was used, the defects would disappear. The defects are described as minor. compared with the advantages the megalopolis has bestowed. The defects brought on by cluster—traffic congestion, slum areas, air and water polution—are viewed as controllable if technology were applied. John Jackson states that technology has within its power the ability to overcome any of the above "annoyances" to urban living which detract from the quality of living in urban environments. He adds that this could be accomplished in a span of thirty years, if there were a real desire.[2] Jane Jacobs, the urban utopian, supports this view:

> The vital cities are not helpless to combat even the most difficult problems. They are not passive victims of chains of circumstances any more than they are the malignant opposite of nature. Vital cities have marvelous abilities for understanding, communicating, contriving, and inventing what is required to combat their difficulties. The surplus, the talents that permit society to support advances, such as conquering disease, are themselves products of our organization into cities.[3]

The fact of the matter is that these defects are endemic and integral to large conurbations. The time and funds spent in determining new and better palliatives could be saved if more experts acknowledged a basic structural imbalance. Beyond a certain point, as a city grows in size and complexity, the initial advantages of urban living (convenience, mobility, and production) begin to go in reverse; and disadvantages (noise, overcrowding, neurosis, crime, and fear) increase.

Another factor that reemphasizes that the cluster is obsolete is the dependence of the metropolis on oil. The clustering itself is in part due to and made possible by cheap and the once-held view of unlimited resources of fossil fuel. The population in the cluster form is built upon a precarious foundation of complicated interdependence. Oil has allowed individual vehicles to run at will and caused sprawl. If overnight, oil supplies were cut in half, the metropolis would be crippled. While it is doubtful that any change in oil supply will be that abrupt, the gradual increase in price which will accompany dwindling supplies will hasten migration from cluster, which in turn will modify the urban transportation habits and accelerate the move to nonmetropolitan areas.

Clustering in the form of a metropolis tends to standardize values and life-styles. The metropolitan life-style we have created has the potentiality to obliterate other forms. The spread-out megalopolis envisioned by Doxiodis[4] and others should not be the only environment our civilization produces. The specter of homogeneity discourages challenge, stimuli, and creativity.

Many utopian urbanologists continue to prescribe traditional remedies. Institutions are rarely changed until their possibilities have been largely exhausted. By undertaking an in-depth review and analysis of structural imbalances, deceptive abstractions can be avoided, and smooth transitions to new institutions can be made.

One can only begin by suggesting the changes that are taking place. Cluster of any kind is a result of a cost of transporting something. If the cost of transport were zero, we would expect activity of all kinds to be uniformly spread over space. Lowering transport costs inevitably reduces clustering and increases dispersion. Due to advances in transportation technology, the influence and significance of geographic distance and geographic place are rapidly declining. The exclusive interaction with geographic neighbors is from a bygone age. That age maintained social communities wherein economics and politics were structured about a place. Today's structures of space have rapidly eroded due to a modern travel and communication industry removing a city from its unique function as an urbanizing instrument of society.

The other attribute of clusters which is slowly disappearing is tolerance of other life-styles born of cultural interchange among diverse citizenry. As clusters have grown, we have seen the metropolis segregated by race and income. Denied a focal point for interaction with a diverse population, the urban resident remains within his racially and economically homogeneous neighborhood. The former opportunity for human interaction took place in the compact city and neighborhood centers which allowed the intermingling of all types of human activities in close proximity. This opportunity for human action is lacking in the spread, centerless metropolis. America has virtually ceased creating new settlements of the traditional type, with stores, offices, schools, and churches closely linked by sidewalks. Instead, we scatter these elements of community along channels of transportation, wherever they are convenient. We create linear cities, or road towns, settlements without centers. While we can get quickly from place to place, we have no place to sit and watch the flow of human events, to meet new people. Thus in the sense that our modern metropolis does not encourage the human encounter, in the sense that it tends to herd homogeneous groups into separated economic and cultural areas, in the sense that public life is stifled, the life-style within may be termed degrading. Beyond its implications for everyday life, such cultural homogenization may prevent the full development of human potentiality. René Dubos comments:

> One can take it for granted that latent potentialities have a better chance to become actualized when the social environment is sufficiently diversified to provide a variety of stimulating experiences, especially for the young. As more persons find the opportunity to express more completely their biological endowment, society becomes richer; and civilizations continue to unfold. By contrast, when the surroundings and way of life are highly stereotyped, the only components on man's nature that flourish are those adapted to the narrow range of prevailing conditions.[5]

The Myths of Urbanity

There is no dispute that, in the past, clusters attracted the inquisitive, the motivated, and the educated. The control of the communication media, along with a heavy concentration of business headquarters, financial institutions, museums, and theaters, created a one-sided knowledge bank for urbanites. Along with this cultural superiority and diversity, there was an environment of growth. These factors imbued the urbanite with confidence and morale. The fact that he may have attended the latest play or major league baseball game, or discussed the newest skyscraper further accentuated his image of importance. The mere presence or identification with a dynamic area makes the individual feel he is a part of the dynamism. The identity with success is psychologically satisfying. Size qua size has a certain attraction which also engenders an attitude of success. For example, if your city has the largest hotel, brewery, or bawdyhouse, it adds to the imagery of importance.

The fact that the urban resident enjoyed a multifaceted life with cultural and social amenities not available to ruralites and small town residents created a chasm between the country and city and led to an urban stereotype. The stereotype portrayed the urbanite as confident, decisive, intellectual, and enjoying the good life. The good life consisted of a vibrant nightlife, interspersed with stimulating visits to plays and museums. This myth of superiority has been shaped and sustained by the publications and media which are urban-oriented. This image is furthered by advertisements which show the sophisticated, fashionable urban couple standing on an exquisite balcony overlooking the city lights toasting each other with vintage wine.

The superiority complex and urban stereotype of the sophisticated man of action has been shattered by reality. The typical central-city resident is poor and uneducated. The great era of urban growth has ended, and a new era of urban shrinkage has begun. The urban monopoly no longer exists. Modern transportation makes almost everyone within an hour's travel of the unique metropolitan possessions, such as museums, theaters, and major league sports. Dissemination of knowledge, in the form of radio, television, and cassettes, has broken the monopoly hold of urban areas. Art appreciation is not limited to the metropolis. Since 1950, over $560 million has been committed to the construction of 10.2 million square feet at 123 American art museums—the equivalent of 13.2 Louvres.[6] Smaller towns are much like the first suburbs, enjoying such advantages as low density, no pollution, and the amenities of the metropolitan area via easy transportation. The new stereotype of success will see medium-size towns as having friendliness, accessibility to knowledge, and tranquility to savor the good life.

The Pleasure Garden

Since World War II, the average American has been living as if he were in a pleasure garden. René Dubos states that the notion of a pleasure garden assumes that there is plenty of energy, land, and water for all, and that any and all technology should be developed and used to maximize affluence. This metaphor assumes that natural resources should be used for the accommodation of the urban system. An objective measurement of contemporary consumption is the increase in the average annual energy usage in America of 0.8 percent for the 1950s to 2.7 percent in the 1970s, a growth of more than 300 percent.[7] This consumption style is in part due to the acculturation of the West and the ancient view of human dominance over nature. These concepts are joined by an interpretation of free market capitalism, that unfettered growth is good, which in turn justifies the pleasure-garden mentality.[8]

Radical changes are necessary to wean our society from this attitude. The editors of *Blueprint for Survival* spoke out early against industrial progress at all costs.[9] They contend that the central problems of the environment are not occurring merely because of temporary or isolated malfunctions of the economic system. Instead, they are warning signs of the intrinsic instability of a society which measures progress as the growth of the gross national product (GNP). Environmental deterioration can no longer be allowed as a trade-off for industrial progress. These signs must be taken seriously, and society must recognize the earth as a space ship, limited in its resources and vulnerable to thoughtlessness in handling.

The inherent danger of the pleasure-garden mentality is the destruction of the environment, especially in the larger cities. As Dubos reminds us: "Society through social groups that have managed to escape from the world into a pleasure garden have achieved little else and generally have not been permitted to enjoy it for long."[10]

One answer lies in the hope that technology will continue to find solutions in alternative energy sources and pollutant combatants. The most realistic hope, however, is smaller systems. The smaller the city, the less artificial is the environment and the greater its stability. Dispersal of population is a basic ingredient in the application of ecological preservation.

Cosmetics Do Not Work

Critics of dispersal generally believe that a Marshall Plan for the city will restore cities to health. This once refulgent vision of patching the existing metropolis has grown dimmer. The concept of permanent or long-term subsidies will not be accepted by the majority of Americans. The sad fact is that patchwork treatment has not and will not work within the existing structural defects.

Another school of thought is massive cosmetics in the form of a regional city. Scott Greer, in *The Emerging City*, proposed the solution of one big city which is organized, incorporating all the suburbs and urban fringe areas. The new entity would make major decisions on mass transit, highway, and land use which could be coordinated throughout the region. The city would then once again become the encompassing community. Greer believes that because of the high degree of interdependence in our present society that a concentration and an information control center are necessary.[11]

This proposed regional city is destined for failure. Regeneration of cities proposed by Greer is impossible. We cannot go back and restructure the existing metropolitan area into an efficient all-encompassing community. Failure is due in large part to the vastly different viewpoints of the suburban and central-city areas. Their interactions usually cut proposals of governmental reform into a series of paper dolls. Citizens of competing areas look with indifference or anxiety at the merger. Two sets of officials with individual vested interests see nothing but danger, loss, and self-destruction in a merger. Partisanship for each area is based on diverse feelings. The general sentiment in the suburb is that they will be invaded by city ills, and continual separation is a continuing desire. Any compromise or dissipation of power to a regional entity is given short shrift by most of the affected political units. City residents who control the central area still retain a quasi-leadership role, and the political transfer to a regional unit is the conveyance of one of the last proprietary rights of the central city. City renewal, if it is not made part and parcel of a comprehensive reorganization of the whole structure of settlement on a large scale, is fantasy.

Along with continued pleas for the regional city, the renewal and preservation of the core area has become a pet ambition of numerous mayors and city planning advisers. They seem to be insensitive to the grave implication this policy involves. A good portion of the central city is deadweight. The causes and not the symptoms should be attacked. Aimless urban renewal for poor and uneducated citizens in the worst living environment in the country simply increases the problem at a high social cost. The problems of the ghetto simply cannot be solved based on a structure where millions of residents with low incomes and other significant disadvantages are required or persuaded to live together in the ghetto.

The disturbing feature of the urban cosmetologist is his wild abandon in the use of public funds. The "throwing some money at a problem" philosophy has become too persuasive. Charles Abrams unbelievably states: "In a nation whose affections for cities is inconspicuous, it makes no sense to scuttle any program, however imperfect, that aims to help them."[12]

Conclusion

Modern technology not only permits us to disperse, but also demands that we do or die of urban strangulation. Dispersal is occurring, without direction other than force of circumstance.

Large-scale systems are vulnerable because of their rigidity. Lest we invest too heavily in a single structure, we may find our ability to respond effectively to new challenges compromised. It is often difficult in America to admit mistakes, to shift gears openly, or to stop misguided programs when vested interests have been accommodated. The inexorable march to metropolis will come to a halt, and statesmen with foresight will openly espouse dispersal.

The historical impetus to conglomeration has reached its zenith, and the pendulum is swinging to the concept of dispersal. The first indication of urban discontent was noted early in our country by the growth of suburbs. This development provided a certain isolation and remoteness from urban reality. Many suburbs, however, now suffer the same maladies which had originally been left behind in the city: intensity, density, pollution, and congestion.

What some planners foresee is another megalopolis such as New York. It is frightening: the same thing we have today only more of it. It is the wrong route. A large-scale urban system will be challenged continually in the future under allegations that it inhibits democracy and degrades the natural environment. The fact that most urbanologists foresee the increased conglomeration of large-scale urban systems, along with their so-called advantages of privacy and mobility, ensures a vigorous debate on the dispersal issue.

The Implementation of Dispersal

We shape our buildings, and afterwards, our buildings shape us. —Winston Churchill

The implementation of the concept of dispersal requires the acknowledgment and awareness of two major forces in America. One is the inalienable right of locational preference, and the second is the inefficacy of professional planning.

The freedom to live where one desires is as important to Americans as the right of an individual to own property. Freedom of movement is the direct counterpoint to totalitarian restrictions on travel and location of residence. The fact that this right to move is withheld in many parts of the world makes its possession especially cherished in America. In America if one's environment is unsatisfactory, he need not adjust, he is free to leave. Restrictions on migration have been constrained by the general conviction that the freedom to move around the country is a virtually unconditional personal right.

The proponent of dispersal must also be cognizant of the extant power and influence of professional planners. Even when planners realize that dispersal is both logical and beneficial to our nation, their plans and support will in all probability have little impact. Implementation will occur only when individual Americans perceive that dispersal will improve their quality of life. To pin hopes on the unctions of the planner is imprudent when one considers his track record. City planners often operate in a gadfly role to the world of privatism. Masterful and resourceful plans are laid out at town meetings. Elected officials are ostensibly impressed with the concept. The planner in his esoteric language explains the function and parameters of his concepts. Then special-interest groups and the affected lobbies react and explain why the plan is unrealistic in its particular impact on their constituency. The political interests then require a compromise from the planner so as to water down or obviate the goal he sought. It is this compromise that makes the city planner subordinate to the power structure.

Planners often seem to be the antithesis of laissez-faire. The fact that planners place constraints on business or forbid them to locate where they prefer puts them at loggerheads with the business community. The planners often are categorized as opponents to the private decision-making process. This slur often proves to be fatal to the implementation of planning. Even when planning is identified as an orderly, systemized method of obtaining an agreed-upon goal, Americans have not been receptive.

The dispersalist must tread a careful path, not placing undue hope in dispersal coming from the top in the form of a plan. The dispersalist, when alleged to be a new type of planner, must emphasize that he is proposing no restrictions on locational preference and that freedom of movement will continue to be unfettered.

Acknowledging these constraints and traditions, how is the concept of dispersal to be implemented? This chapter defines the policy of dispersal, reviews governmental endorsement, perceives the beginning of a spontaneous dispersal, and emphasizes the necessity of continued education of the public.

Policy of Dispersal

1. Whereas the citizens of this country remain dedicated to the proposition that each individual shall have an inalienable right to move at will.
2. Whereas American cities have reached population levels which are harmful to the general welfare in the form of social density, lack of citizen participation, pollution, and economic inefficiency.
3. Whereas America has reached the age and maturity where population distribution has become a national concern and a subject of study for all interested citizens.
4. Whereas the greatest health, welfare, and dignity for the greatest number is the essence of Americans' heritage and creed.

Now therefore, the following policy of dispersal is hereafter set forth:

1. The citizens of this country shall henceforth signify that the quality of life and environmental preservation be of top domestic priority.
2. A national policy to encourage intermediate-size cities and rural areas as growth centers be advocated by the executive and legislative branches of the government.
3. The implementation of this policy shall involve balanced federal aid between metropolitan areas, medium-size growth centers, and rural areas, along with the designation by states of preferred growth areas within the state's boundaries.
4. A national commission on population distribution should be created to establish goals for balanced growth and to provide the latest demographic findings to be publicized and distributed to the public.[1] As part of the dissemination of this information, job-bank counseling centers should be located in areas of high unemployment and underemployment.

Government and Dispersal

The urban explosions of the 1960s focused attention on conditions in the cities. As reports and studies were completed, there appeared to be a connection between the migration from the poor, rural areas and the tensions which surfaced in the city. Political leaders expressed concern and attempted to alleviate the problems by a burst of manpower and job retraining bills, which became known as the Johnson war on poverty legislation. Although legislative proposals on structural revisions and population control were sparse, there were legislative proposals that considered population imbalances which adversely affected both rural and urban areas.

In 1967 Senator Carl Mundt introduced a proposal calling for a National Commission on Balanced Economic Development and stated:

> The sponsors of the resolution suspect that two established trends of today, and the considerable problems resulting from each of the trends, are not separate but are rather parts of one problem—how to achieve a balanced national economic development.
>
> We suspect that the deepening problems of the cities result in part from too sudden and too great a concentration of population. We suspect some cities have passed the point of diminishing returns in the growth and concentration of population. The cost of public services, transportation, government, and day-to-day living exceed the levels which might prevail under more efficient conditions of population concentration.[2]

In 1968, for the first time, both political parties recognized the problem and made promises. This dual source is reflected in their contrasting statements. The Republican declaration came under the heading "Crisis of the Cities: success with urban problems in fact requires an acceleration of rural development in order to stem the flow of people from the countryside to the city." The Democratic pledges were under the heading "Rural Development: balanced growth is essential for American . . . to achieve that balanced growth, we must greatly increase the growth of the rural nonfarm economy."[3]

In 1968 the National Governors' Conference found that "the population balance is at the core of nearly every major problem facing our nation today" and urged policies to bring about "a more even distribution of population among the states."[4] In 1969 the National League of Cities called for "a specific policy for the settlement of people throughout the nation to balance the concentration of popoulation among and within metropolitan and nonmetropolitan areas while providing social and economic opportunities for all persons."[5] During 1969 the National Committee on Urban Growth Policy urged the United States to undertake to build 110 new towns to accommodate 20 million citizens.[6]

In January 1970 President Nixon called for an urban growth policy in his State of the Union Address. He stated:

> I proposed . . . the nation develop a national growth policy. In the future, government decisions as to where to build highways, locate airports, acquire land, or sell land should be made with a clear objective of aiding a balanced growth for America. In particular, the federal government must be in a position to assist in the building of new cities and the rebuilding of old ones.[7]

The first legislative action on balanced growth came in 1970 when two statutes were passed, one created the Economic Development Administration, and the second set forth reporting requirements. The Urban Growth and New Community Development Act of 1970 required a report from the Executive Department on Urban Growth, to be delivered in February of each even-numbered year. The first biannual report to Congress, in February 1972, offered little beyond a review of the growth trends and problems that had already been well defined.[8]

During the 1970s, the political leadership backed away from even encouraging population distribution. The Nixon Administration in 1974 stated:

> The objective of encouraging a more even population distribution is not considered to be a valid objective for a federal program at this time. If states desire more even population distributions, the states themselves could decide on policies and incentives for redistribution with the state. Most of the time a competitive, private-decision economy that effectively utilizes its capacity to produce will provide a geographic and functional distribution of people, activities, and resources that is more efficient and desirable than alternative methods.[9]

Congressional leadership also has been dormant on the question of defining a national growth policy or, for that matter, discussing whether such a policy is needed. The rhetoric of 1968 and 1972 was in large part in response to the urban unrest of that period. Heavy media treatment of the cities slowly dissipated. The crisis was in fact given benign neglect, and population growth and distribution policy stirred little interest. This gap in policy is due in large part to a phenomenon known as *reactive incrementalism*.

Reactive incrementalism in government is responsible for the lack of a national policy on population dispersal. The term *reactive incrementalism* is based on the observation that the United States has very little long-term policy. Instead we as a nation tend to react to events with small increments of legislation. Formulation of overall national goals is inhibited because goals or objectives involve planning. American ideology rebels against governmental planning.

In order for legislative or executive action to occur, articulation of a discontent must be communicated, picked up by the media, and widely disseminated.

Second, a large portion of the population must be irritated enough by the problems that they become a top priority issue. This widespread problem must be precisely identified and followed closely by the proposed resolution. Another requisite in obtaining legislative action for the solution is simplicity. If the solution to the problem is complicated and right, it will not be as acceptable as a seemingly reasonable and relatively simple solution. The combination of simplicity and patent rectitude usually wins public support. Although so-called simple solutions usually require a high degree of sophistication and often become complex in implementation, at the outset these complexities must be kept to a minimum.

Any significant legislative proposal by the government arouses public clamor by the group whose vested interest is being affected. The size of this group is very important. If a large unified group is adversely affected, a persistent campaign against the legislation makes the passage difficult. Sheer repetitive denouncement can be an effective defensive tool in blunting legislative initiatives. An small affected group is less likely to block legislative action.

How does the explanation of the above legislative realism apply to population dispersal? Since dispersal is in the interest of the total citizenry, the average citizen fails to perceive or appreciate the concept. Further, he does not believe it will strongly affect him. As a result, the level of political strength has been puerile at best. The fact is that the interests of the defined group are not identical, and the failure to explain dispersal in a simple, clear-cut policy has negated legislative strength. Also the failure to pinpoint an enemy or scapegoat to rally the cause has slowed legislative pronouncements on dispersal.

The proponents of dispersal are on the periphery and ironically are themselves dispersed, which is a deficit start. There is no grave public complaint, no identifiable group, and a geographical solidarity is missing. Up to this point, pragmatic legislators who see no votes in dispersal and who will be alleged to be craven of heart by traditional urban interests have taken little or no interest. The policy of dispersal has usually been left to planners and professors who are generally characterized as utopian and socialistic.

Changes, however, are occurring in conditions, functions, and images of urban areas which make policy or even legislation more possible than ever before. It cannot be denied that the great urban expansion was in large part responsible for rural depletion and the brain drain in medium-size towns. This did not escape public notice, and the policy statements on the rural to urban phenomenon linked the depletion with the growth. These policy statements made small waves for two reasons. First, the urban media gave the interconnection little publicity and, second, there appeared no reason to slow the migration which brought great economic expansion to the urban areas.

Today we have an inflected urban growth curve, terminal areas in central cities, municipal bankruptcies, and a majority of urban citizenry dissatisfied with their residence. A new linkage between central cities and medium-sized growth centers may evolve. This linkage will be forged by the relocation of the excess labor pool to smaller towns.

It is imperative that Americans be emancipated from the commonly assumed view that there is an inexorable march to more and more megalopolises. An open espousal of a specified, defined dispersal policy is required. It is a fact that Americans have more toleration of policy statements than legislative fiats, and this is not a surprise. The expounding of a policy is usually less obtrusive and is often of an ethereal nature. A policy statement, being an expression of a goal or a desired future state of affairs, does not directly affect citizens and is thus tolerated. Therefore dispersal proposals should take the form of policy statements or white papers in the beginning. This dignified entry into the public forum creates both an aura of respectability and the base for future criticism or support. Reports by commissions on urban violence, pornography, and energy have been accorded different degrees of acceptance. However, their impact on the national psyche cannot be denied. These reports are also important as reference material for future studies or legislation.

The exposure of a concept or policy to the glare of public scrutiny often has a leavening effect. Every person has a view on the subject of city size and preference, along with the multifaceted social problems which are inherently linked to city size. The conversation and media treatment of such a broad-based subject would create a topic for dinner-table discussion. Public debate of a subject in a democracy often initiates a certain momentum toward action. The media is the medium; the environment is the formulator.

The subject of population redistribution without coercion is awaiting the day when its importance is recognized. It is evident that there is untapped public concern and an increasing awareness of the implications of population distribution. For example, in 1972 the Commission on Population Growth in the American Future asked, "Do you feel the population distribution is a serious problem, a problem but not so serious, or no problem at all?" About 54 percent of those questioned expressed the opinion that population distribution was indeed a serious problem, 30 percent said that it was not a particularly serious problem, and only 9 percent thought it was no problem at all. The remaining 7 percent of the respondents had no opinion.[10]

The same survey also examined the public's perception of the future importance of population distribution relative to population growth. Those interviewed were asked: "Over the next thirty years, which do you think will be a greater problem—population growth or where people live?" The general public was fairly evenly divided in terms of which problem thay saw as preeminent throughout the rest of the century. About 39 percent chose population growth, but 36 percent considered distribution the more important problem. An additional question asked in this survey was: "Do you think the federal government should discourage or should not discourage further growth of large metropolitan areas?" Nationally, 52 percent of those questioned favored federal action designed to slow the growth of large metropolitan areas; about one-third opposed such action, and the remainder expressed no opinion.[11]

Spontaneous Movement

The implementation of dispersal appears to be occurring spontaneously in the United States. The historic migration flow from rural and small towns to metropolitan areas has reversed. Demographic experts, however, warn that a trend which has turned suddenly downward could turn upward once again. However, the fact that population has stabilized and nonfarm jobs are increasing more rapidly in small towns than in large centers tends to support the view that this reversal will have duration. Calvin L. Beale, the U.S. Department of Agriculture's authority on rural demography, believes that the new tendencies of the 1970s—so radically different from those of the country's whole previous history—have come to stay. Beale states:

> Essentially, every current trend in residential preferences, business location decisions, land use, effect on affluence, closure of comparative differences in the facilities and amenities of rural and urban areas, supports rural and small city growth. . . . It is essential for policymakers and the public in general to realize that the curve of rural and non-metropolitan population trends have inflected. The factors that impelled out-migration in the midcentury years have lost most of their force. A new perspective is needed.[12]

If the above is in fact a long-term phenomenon, there is a question of whether population dispersal policies are needed. Even if the spontaneous reversal continues, a national policy is intrinsically desirable. The phenomenon will tend to create parochial views. Spokesmen for urban interests may have supported national dispersal policies when the metropolitan area was thriving and expanding. However, as actual shrinkage of large cities becomes a reality, antagonism between urban interests and dispersalists could result.

A second group to consider is the small city politicians who have attempted to limit population in small, fast-growing communities. They have done so in high-growth communities in Colorado, California, and Florida. While this group can understand the dispersal and appreciate its benefits on a generalized basis, they fight the onslaught of great numbers into their towns on the grounds that their present environment would drastically change.

Public Education

As the policy of dispersal becomes an issue of debate, the education and therewith the concepts of the young will be decisive. Today's young American is often better informed than his parents. As tedious subsistence living becomes rarer, the consideration of one's life-style becomes the essential concern. The mobility that is accepted by the younger generation has created options which were unimaginable to prior generations. The mental processes that underline the selection of a life-style will place a greater and greater emphasis on the quality of life. The bare quantitative conception of living is being challenged by a more comprehensive consideration. The distaste for the large corporation and the dislike of size qua size is no longer concealed. This change is developing throughout the population more rapidly than commonly assumed. The 1950s and 1960s city of tomorrow was an urban scene of concrete and self-contained building communities. That city of the future was a mass of intertwined highways with cloverleafs, a la Los Angeles. This picture would be vehemently rejected by today's university students if presented as the utopian city of tomorrow. The Tom Corbet, spaceman, concept, envisaging concrete cities far removed from any greenery is ludicrous. This vision of progress is sterile and unacceptable.

The constant neurotic striving for greater scale, spiraling consumption, planned obsolescence, creation of new products to fulfill created but unneeded demands will wane. The educated are coming to see wisdom in the intermediate technology school and the small is beautiful concepts of E.F. Schumacher.[13] The small community can provide stability and will be the city of tomorrow.

Another factor of great import is the decline of achievement and financial success as the idol or salvation of mankind. The domination of the economy by the large corporations is creating a new security-oriented employee for which family raising, environment, and climate are becoming as important as more spendable dollars. The media, while still dominated by the latest car style, is becoming more alert to a generation interested in life-styles of contentment rather than competition.

Conclusion

The implementation of dispersal has history on its side. The shortage of fossil fuel and the turnaround in population migration to smaller towns are uncontroverted facts. The migration from the metropolis occurring in present-day America renders dispersal as a reality rather than a wispy utopian hope built upon a radical change in human nature. The discernment by business that profitable markets are in intermediate-size growth centers and that employees desire to work there will provide additional momentum for dispersal. The perception that quality of life is not antithetical to material growth, and that nonmetropolitan living will allow both, will further encourage dispersal.

Although dispersal appears to be beginning spontaneously, future urbanization requires a planning policy. The scale of interdependence and technology today requires a vision extending well into the future. Planning of urbanization has up to this stage been based on a concept of concentration along with continued growth and widespread affluence. These versions must be challenged and analyzed. The above blend of strategies will result in public debate that will affect the existing structural entity. The emergence of the dispersal issue will force political leaders to take a position. To date, no significant public figure has urged the implementation of such a policy with the fervor and urgency it deserves. The implementation of dispersal will not come without initial confrontation with metropolitan vested interests. The idea of rejuvenated outlying communities attracting large numbers is still dismissed as unrealistic by many urbanologists. As dispersal takes place, it may be accused of causing the stagnation of large cities, which in fact is caused by overclustering. In reality, a thinning or pruning of the metropolitan population will have a benign effect.

5

The Seeds of
Dispersal

We will ever strive for the ideals and sacred things of the city, both alone and with many; we will unceasingly seek to quicken the sense of public duty; we will revere and obey the city laws; we will transmit the city not less, but greater, better, and more beautiful than it was transmitted to us.—Oath of the Athenian state

The Proposals of Ebenezer Howard

Ebenezer Howard, a modest English court reporter, originally planted the seeds of dispersal in the 1890s. His proposals were a reaction against the great industrial revolution influx of the masses into London. Howard's writing dealt with the quality of life, city size, and the physical environment.

Although Howard has never been accorded personal historical significance, his writings must be regarded as classics in the field of urban planning. He has been termed the utopian visionary, a myopic and fearful businessman, a compromiser, a radical, a harmless intellectual, and a destroyer of cities. The central expression of his thesis was published in 1898 in his *Garden Cities of Tomorrow*.[1] This book has been reviewed by a wide range of urban analysts and is usually noted with a high degree of praise or scorn, depending on the interpretation and philosophy of the reviewer. Howard's reputation has been further confused by the use of his term *garden city* in association with urban forms antithetical or at marked variance from his own beliefs. This barrage of criticism, praise, and confusion results in the fact that Howard's ideas are now obscured. Since he was one of the first in the industrial era to write a serious proposal for alternative urban forms, his work deserves consideration on its own merits.

Ebenezer Howard was born in London in 1850, the son of a small shopkeeper. He had, as F.J. Osborn notes, "no special advantages of class or education," and was never a wealthy man.[2] His formal education ended when he was 14 years old and he had no special training in architecture or design. At 21, he went to America where he took up state land in Nebraska and attempted farming. Unhappy and unsuccessful, he moved to Chicago where he became a court reporter. He returned to England in 1876, joined a firm of parliamentary reporters, and devoted himself to his family, his mechanical inventions, and his social proposals. His travels provided the essential background and stimulus for his work. He observed firsthand the squalor and congestion of the industrial city, the abandonment of rural areas, the lack of a real community, and the

beginnings of urban sprawl. He was especially influenced by Edward Bellamy's
Looking Backward, which was a vision of Boston in the year 2000.[3]

Frederick Osborn, who along with Lewis Mumford has been Howard's
prime champion, reminds us that Howard was not a political theorist, but an
inventor.[4] An inventor does not formulate new ideas, but combines existing
ones in a new way. Howard experimented with a wide range of ideas until he
found a combination of proposals. He never listed these as such, instead devot-
ing himself to explanatory rhetoric. He was an earnest and practical man who
was concerned lest his schemes be dismissed as too practical or utopian. Despite
Howard's effort to make his proposal economical and pleasing to the populace
and businessmen of the time, his scheme *was* radical for its time and in its pure
form is radical in view of contemporary urban forms.

Howard proposed the creation of a new kind of city, a new kind of metropolitan area, a new system of land controls, and a new system of government.
His new city was, as he termed it, a marriage of town and country. The town,
with its excitement, high wages, and employment opportunities, suffered from
high prices and poor-living conditions. The beauty of the countryside was
hampered by its economic backwardness and lack of amusement. Howard
described his proposal by simply showing a diagram of three magnets, each
with its particular drawing power, its particular accommodation of attraction
and repulsion (figure 5-1).

The task of the planner was to create the new city which would have high
wages and low rents. In the diagram, people are pulled like iron filings by each
of the magnets. This aspect of the metaphor is to show that people will respond
freely and rationally to the environment which gives them the most advantages.
It is not a difficult notion to understand. However, it has often been wrongfully
interpreted to mean a mixture of urban and rural qualities, a mixture which
would produce a suburban hodgepodge destroying the unique advantages of
both town and country. In fact, Howard's garden city is directly antithetical
to suburban sprawl. He proposed that each city be built upon a 5,000-acre
tract surrounded by an agricultural greenbelt. The garden city is planned,
limited in size, independent, united with agriculture, and endowed with
social purpose. These characteristics, which do not apply to suburbs, deserve
some further exploration.

Howard stated the necessity for planning as follows: "It is essential . . . that
there should be unity of design and purpose—that the towns should be planned
as a whole and not left to grow up in a chaotic manner as is the case with all
English towns, and more or less so with the towns of all countries."[5]

Howard's firm belief in planning is often confused with the endorsement
of a particular kind of design. In fact, his was a social experiment, not a physical
one. His ideas on design are always qualified with such statements as "this
might be a good form." He was not a designer, and his ideas on the subject
may well be regarded as merely suggestions. What is important is the social

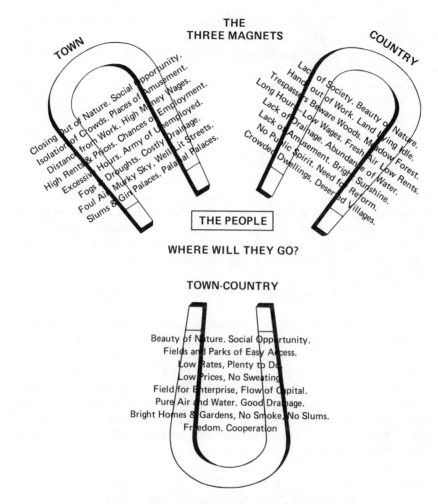

Source: Ebenezer Howard, *Garden Cities of Tomorrow* (1898; definitive ed., Cambridge, Mass.: MIT Press, 1946). Reprinted with permission

Figure 5-1. Three Magnets of Ebenezer Howard

implications of planning, and the most crucial of these is public control of town size.

Howard conceived the city as an organic, balanced, interrelated unit, whose social benefits and functional productivity would decrease if the city grew too large. This is a very old idea, in fact a classical idea. Osborn notes that "The Greeks accepted in theory and practice the limitation of the population-size of a city-state . . . [This idea of limits] was held by Lycurgus of Sparta (820 B.C.), Solon of Athens (ca. 640-558 B.C.). Plato evolved the formula of 5,040 families (not counting retainers and slaves), and was criticized by Aristotle for putting the figure too high."[6]

Lewis Mumford comments that such limits did "not merely prevent congestion, but maintained a balance between town and country that may have been one of the conditions that fostered the extraordinary creativity of the Hellenistic Age."[7] Another example of classical roots may be found in the ideas of Leonardo da Vinci, who proposed distributing the citizens of congested sixteenth-century Milan into ten cities of 30,000 each.[8]

In the industrial age, such ideas were largely forgotten. Growth of cities was seen as a sign of prosperity and a source of pride. Such pride in growth is symbolic of the change in purpose of the city from social to economic. Mumford writes: "The uncontrolled growth of the city was looked upon as proof of its value for civilization. That the mechanical and financial agents of our civilization might be managed in the public interest, that it might be wiser to build new towns of limited extent than to overcrowd and overextend old ones was not treated even as a theoretical possibility before the end of the nineteenth century."[9]

This is a crucial point. Howard is often classified as an archenemy of cities, one who would break them up and destroy their vitality. Actually, he was one of the few thinkers of his time to seriously formulate and praise the social purposes of cities. His essential point was that these human purposes could not be fulfilled as the city grew beyond a manageable human-scaled size. Recognizing that no small city could achieve the technological and cultural diversity of large cities, Howard proposed the "creation of a regional unit that would bring into a single, organized system at least ten cities with a total transportation system." Within this regional system the principle of limits to growth remains inviolate. Each single city functions as a self-controlled community; each is separated from the others by a municipally owned belt of rural land.

The provision of a greenbelt surrouding the city is not meant for the sole purpose of limiting the city's growth, though that is one of its intentions. Howard meant the greenbelt to be used for agriculture as an integral part of the city. His term *garden city* is properly defined as a city set in productive gardens; not, as many interpreted, as a city containing beautiful lawns. The landbelt was intended to provide the benefits of closer markets and town access to the farmers and cheaper food prices, convenient disposal of refuse and sewage, and access to rustic beauty for the town dwellers. Howard wrote:

> The combination of town and country is not only helpful but economic. Consider vegetables and fruits. Farmers, except near towns, do not often grow them now. Why? Chiefly because of the difficulty and uncertainty of a market, and the high charges for freights and commissions.[10]

The placing of markets near centers of production serves to enhance the economic security of the small farmer, thus preserving a traditional life-style, and saving energy in the distribution of produce. The farmers in the greenbelt are part of the garden city where they lease municipally owned land; but the rural isolation is not threatened by urban sprawl. The garden city is a rigorously confined urban grouping. Rather than scattering the population over agricultural lands, it organizes them into compact communities. Howard recommended town densities of approximately thirty persons to the acre, a figure which is higher than most metropolitan areas in the United States. The density was for the preservation of agriculture and open land.

Frederick Osborn notes that the greenbelt has historic roots which go back to biblical times:

> Foreshadowings of Howard's ideas are many. Perhaps the oldest is the layout prescribed for the cities of Palestine (circa thirteenth century B.C.). This idea of pasture lands around a town . . . is evidenced by the proposals of Ezekiel for the layout of Jerusalem seven centuries later (592-570 B.C.). A century and a half later (circa 444 B.C.) Nehemiah's accounting of his building of the walls of the holy city, on his spell of leave from captivity in Persia, shows that these agricultural reservations were still respected. The intervening dispersal into the countryside was regarded as a fall from grace.[11]

The idea that town and country should embody distinct environments and life-styles recurs throughout history and is found in a form strikingly similar to Howard's in Thomas Moore's *Utopia* (A.D. 1516).[12] Osborn provides this synopsis:

> Sir Thomas Moore's *Utopia* closely approaches Howard's "garden city" pattern. The 54 cities of *Utopia* were 20 or more miles apart, and there is both a distinction and relationship between town and country . . . the chief city is two miles square, walled, and with a sort of green belt around the walls—not for military purposes, since it is overgrown with briars, etc., but as an intermediate zone between town and country.[13]

Howard also sought to maintain a distinction between town and country, though he did want to provide the residents of each with ready access to the other. As a practical man, he saw the distinction would best be preserved in unity. Unless the farmland was united with and protected by the municipality, it would be threatened by urban sprawl. This notion must be distinguished from a mixture of town and country, which is associated with suburban landscape. The garden city in Howard's theory was meant to unify town and country in a regional system but to preserve the distinct environments of each.

Howard's garden-city proposal included public ownership of land wherein land users would enter into long-term leases. His political ideas, however, are clearly subservient to the overall purpose of the creation of order and design. In many ways, this is a humane order. Howard was struck by the economic inefficiency and human waste of unemployment; he detested the congestion and squalor which characterized the cities of his time. He abhorred oppression of the working class; he was fearful of the ruination of rustic beauty by chaotic sprawl. His own expression of his central purpose in promulgating the garden city may be best interpreted as a humane desire to counter the more chaotic and oppressive aspects of the industrial revolution. As he stated:

> The object of the garden city: to find for our industrial population work at wages of higher purchasing power, and to secure healthier surroundings and more regular employment . . . its object is, in short, to raise the standard of health and comfort of all true workers of whatever grade . . . the means by which these objects are to be achieved being a healthy, natural, and economic combination of town and country life, and this on land owned by the municipality.[14]

Howard's genius was not only the conceptualization of the garden-city plan but also the construction of such a city. In 1898 he had to borrow £50 to print his publication *Garden Cities of Tomorrow*. Five years later his supporters were advancing £100 to begin the construction of the first garden city. Another unique facet to the Howard story is that he looked only to voluntary groups for backing. He resisted the temptation to make the garden city a matter of party politics and to seek state funds to build the prototype. Although Howard continually attempted to obtain working-class support, he ended up aligning himself with two industrial magnates to obtain financial resources for the garden city. George Cadbury, the chocolate magnate, and W.H. Lever, the soap merchant, provided the initial financial support. Both men had previously built company towns characterized by open layout and ample green spaces, to house their workers.[15]

Howard was an optimistic man. He felt that people would rejoice in order and accept control. He believed that the placing of residences in settings of natural beauty would relieve the negative aspects of work in the industrial era. He held that an integrated, cooperative, exciting community would evolve naturally, given only the proximity of nature. He believed that if his scheme were economically feasible, it would be readily accepted by his countrymen. As shown later, Howard's theory became a reality in the form of the English new towns.

Critics of Ebenezer Howard

From the very beginning, Howard's theory was dismissed as impossible and impractical. In 1898 the *Fabian News* contained an editorial which stated:

His plans would have been in time if they had been submitted to the Romans when they conquered Britain. They set about laying out cities, and our forefathers have dwelled in them to this day. Now Mr. Howard proposes to pull them all down and substitute garden cities, each duly built according to pretty colored plans, nicely designed with a ruler and compass. The author has read many learned and interesting writers, and the extracts he makes from their books are like plums in the impalpable dough in his utopian scheme. We've got to make the best of our existing cities, and proposals for building new ones are about as useful as would be arrangements for protection against visits from Mr. Welles' martians.[16]

Historian Murray Bookchin criticized Howard as follows:

In Howard's work, design was assigned the task of achieving sweeping goals that actually involve revolutionary changes in the entire economic, social and cultural fabric of bourgeois society.... It leaves undefined the nature of human contiguity, community, and the relationship between the urban dweller and the natural world. Most important, it leaves undefined the nature of work, the control of means of production, the problem of distributing goods and services equitably and the conflicting social interests that collect around these issues ... Howard's garden cities of tomorrow are permeated by an underlying assumption ... that a compromise can be struck between the intrinsically irrational material reality and a moral ideology of high-minded conciliation.[17]

Bookchin considers Howard's dependence on design as simplistic, chides him for not radically challenging capitalism, and asserts that he laid the framework for the modern suburb.

The fact that Howard did not critique the capitalistic system and openly embrace socialism can be attributed to his pragmatism. He intentionally moderated his social views so that he would not antagonize the very people he needed to support and invest in his garden community. Further, it is unfair to evaluate Howard as solely dependent on design. While design is the main thrust, he expounds on the integration of agriculture and explains self-government and control as integral components of his proposed town. Howard admired civilization as it is associated with the polis, civic consciousness, and the flowering of individual potential. Further, the assertion that Howard spawned or advocated the suburban form of today is wrong. He would be appalled at the omission of the greenbelt and at the nonindependent dense suburbs which are contiguous to every major metropolis.

E.A. Gutkind states that garden cities have the inherent ailment of cultural, social, and economic dependence on nearby large cities.[18] While such dependence may be characterized by garden cities as they exist today, it was certainly not Howard's aim. He sought to reverse the trend of concentration. His proposal was a complete dispersal of society into small, self-contained communities separated by greenbelts and linked by rapid transit.

Jane Jacobs, in *Death and Life of Great American Cities,* accuses Howard of setting forth city-destroying ideas. She maintains that his focus on housing and his design of city zones for specific uses are sterile. Jacobs opines that cosmopolitanism, diversity, and excitement have been drained from the Howardian towns.[19] The simple environment proposed by Howard, while considered as destructive of stimulating atmosphere by Jacobs, continues to be the hope of the majority of urban residents as shown by the latest surveys on living preference. The use of zones for specific uses in various neighborhoods and urban areas has been widely adopted in America. This designation of land use is in accord with the order and stability Howard admired.

Conclusion

The unheralded and misinterpreted Howard has set forth a fundamental structural concept which will continue to have far-reaching effects. The last decade has found an increasing number of industrialized countries enacting policies on population growth patterns. Many of these countries are adopting Howard's basic principle.

Howard's proposal was originally conveyed to a world without the auto, telephone, television, or jet travel. His germinal idea has now been nurtured by circumstances which render it more feasible. The continued growth of agglomerations based on archaic industrial requirements makes his proposal more urgent and compelling than it was at the turn of the century.

The wisdom of Howard is shown in his preparation of a simple plan and the fact that it could be implemented within the existing economic system. An intricate proposal combining a radical challenge to capitalism would have merely placed another utopia on dusty library shelves. Pragmatic genius is shown by the rare occurrence of a world-changing proposal which became a reality in his lifetime. Howard's faith and perserverance culminated in the founding of Letchworth and Welwin, the first English new towns.

The New Towns

In the next forty years, we must rebuild the entire urban United States.—Lyndon Baines Johnson

The major response to industrialized megalopolis to date has been the new city proposals. The contribution of Ebenezer Howard included not only a pedagogical concept but also a pragmatism that gave birth to the first English new town.

The English Experience

Ebenezer Howard believed that his garden-city concept could best be proven by demonstration. His first demonstration project was the town of Letchworth, which was started in England by a private development corporation in 1904. The second new town, Welwin, was begun in 1919. The new towns had neither governmental assistance nor endorsement, and the financial backing obtained solely from the private sector was often inadequate. Both, however, managed to attract population and industry on their own merits prior to World War II.[1]

In 1937, a Royal Commission on the Distribution of Industrial Population was established to study the problems of urban overcrowding and industrial concentration in the London area. The result was the Barlow Report, which urged governmental intervention to stop urban sprawl and rural depopulation.[2]

After World War II, the British government was faced with the problem of relocating thousands of people whose homes had been destroyed. During this postwar period Parliament reached the consensus that the unchecked growth of London was undesirable socially, economically, and strategically.

Patrick Abercrombie's Greater London Plan of 1944 sought to contain the growth of London by surrounding it with a greenbelt five-miles wide, and relocating 1.25 million people in an outer ring of satellite suburbs.[3] The greenbelt component of this plan, while appearing revolutionary and radical, had in fact previously been proposed by Elizabeth I (1580) and Oliver Cromwell (1653) who had both attempted to limit the growth of London by encircling it with an enforced greenbelt.[4]

The New Town Act of 1946, a refinement to Abercrombie's original plan, was passed in an attempt to stop the relentless expansion of London. The act outlined the creation of new outer-ring towns. This legislation basically adopted Howard's philosophy of residential and industrial areas in towns with populations of 30,000. Self-contained, socially balanced communities were to provide new population growth in independent towns rather than allow continued growth on the fringes of London. However, in contrast to Letchworth and Welwin, the postwar new towns were heavily subsidized by the government. Sixty-year loans from the National Treasury at below market interest rates were made available. Special provisions were inserted in loans to cover interest due in years before the new town had adequate cash flow to cover debt service. Eminent domain was used to buy land which was frozen at predevelopment prices. The National Treasury paid rent subsidies to tenants along with governmental subsidies to industry to locate in new towns.[5]

Recent developments have witnessed revisions and expansions of the New Town Act of 1946. During the 1960s the concept of a modest-size new town of 50,000 to 60,000 has been inflated and altered into various forms; a new town added to an old town, and even the creation of a planned city region for nearly 500,000 people. This planned-city region, while a departure from the New Town Act, is remarkably similar to the essential idea of the Social City first enunciated by Ebenezer Howard in 1898.[6]

Since the British government's paramount goals for the new towns were (1) containment of urban areas, especially London; and (2) population distribution by the creation of housing, in economically self-contained communities; it is fairest to evaluate them first on these limited grounds. On the first score, a certain degree of success is evident to everyone in Britain. Agricultural land and scenic areas have been preserved around the large metropolitan areas. Urban growth has been somewhat organized, and the more ruinous effects of sprawl have been abated. As to the issue of population distribution, including the original new towns of Letchworth and Welwin, Britain now has thirty-one new towns, with a population of approximately 1.4 million people.[7] While this is less than 2 percent of the population of Britain, it has made a significant impact on the cutting edge of population growth.

The growth of London has not abated. Long-distance commuting has developed much like the commuting fields in North America. Although outward growth has sometimes leapfrogged the greenbelt, the basic concepts of the new towns have obtained widespread acceptance in England. Continued urban growth after World War II, manifested by the larger new towns, far surpassed the numbers Howard envisioned. He suggested units of 32,000; British new towns have soared as high as 220,000 (Telford), and many are above 100,000.[8] Howard, of course, envisioned a metropolitan system of linked small cities, along with limited growth, as essential to his garden cities. Instead, the new towns have grown larger and larger, in many cases encroaching on their greenbelts for added development. The push to greater size and variety represents a new phase of English New Town Planning, in which traditional decentralization and housing goals have been superseded by an attempt to have major new town developments play a leading role in the national growth policy.

Overall, the English new town experience must be considered a limited success. In 1972, for example, twelve of the thirteen British new towns started during the 1946-1950 period are showing a profit. Profits from the most profitable twelve new towns are sufficient to cover the deficit of the yet unprofitable seventeen.[9] Although new towns have not succeeded in containing urban growth, they have channeled this growth to a limited extent; and the existence of greenbelts has preserved many amenities of the rural landscape. Although the policy has not been strong enough to counter powerful economic trends, it has succeeded in casting these trends into a more desirable form than chaotic sprawl. The English new town concept has also firmly established itself as a part of the national policy. David Hall, executive director of the British Town and Country Planning Association, made the following statement in 1975:

> The New Towns Program is not a luxury. It is something that we see to be essential to the proper management of our resources and our affairs. To that extent, I would venture to suggest that even if Britain's economic situation gets worse than it is now, we shall nevertheless continue withour new town program.[10]

The American New-Town Experience

The American government has never specifically endorsed a new town policy similar to that of the British government. The American tradition is one of improving the existing cities and isolated experiments with new towns which contained some of Howard's concepts.

Progressives of the 1890s presented various prescriptions to assist the exploding metropolis of that period. The Progressives were sometimes labeled as being anticity; in fact, they were concerned that if a city became too large, all sense of community would vanish and social malaise would take its place. Progressives confirmed the need for good government and a regeneration of civic life. It was thought that this would draw persons of culture back and not abandon the public sphere of metropolitan cities to commercialism and corrupt politics. The crux of the change was to be in politics; the preservation of the integrity of the small locality was thought to encourage a sense of belonging. Further, the importance of local government was emphasized because it fostered civic and political participation.

The Progressives were imbued with a strong sense of moral purpose. Some of them idealized a small town as a place with a sense of community, but just as many attempted to work within the context of the city. William James, John Dewey, Jane Addams, and Robert Park tried to establish a sense of belonging and personal contact within the city by dividing it into neighborhood units.[11] One dominant note in their typically Progressive thinking was opposition to gigantism. Their desire was to cut this vague megalopolis down to manageable size. They did not flee the metropolis for the village, but they wanted to decompose the city to spiritual units which would emulate village life. This is evident in Jane Addams' hope that the settlement house would help fill the urban void,[12] and in Dewey's plea for the revival of localism in his *Public and Its Problems.*[13]

The Progressives were generally urbane men who were dismayed by the lack of traditional urban characteristics in the industrial American city. Very few called for the actual dismantling of the city. The primary impact of the Progressive intellectual thought was recognition of the importance of small units as the basis for democracy in community. One of these small units was the autonomous neighborhood in the big city. John Dewey summed up his philosophy most clearly in the warning: "Unless local communal life can be restored, the public cannot adequately resolve its most urgent problem: define and identify itself."[14]

This intellectual tradition never really developed into a city-planning movement or a plan for organized dispersal, despite the scholarly fervor of its proponents. Its emphasis on small, social units remains largely intellectual, isolated from the actual processes of American urbanization. The basic tenets were a desire for a sense of place, limitations on mindless expansion, and identification of neighborhood units to foster democratic participation. These aims, while important to American tradition and thought, have never been effectively embodied in public policy. Instead, public policy has tended to emphasize and encourage other components of the American tradition: individualism, competition, land speculation, and constant growth. When city planning did become widespread and accepted in the twentieth century, an opportunity to implement some progressive goals became possible. Planning was perhaps highest in attempts to create American new towns. These concepts attempted to achieve many of Ebenezer Howard's communitarian goals. Yet, as will be demonstrated, planning of the American new towns failed to develop the alternative environments which would embody a sense of place and belonging, an active civic life, and relative diversity within a manageable unit.

The first new town in America was Sunnyside, New York. It was meant to be a garden city as described by Ebenezer Howard. Its architect and planner, Clarence Stein, an enthusiastic follower of Howard, conceived of Sunnyside as a social as well as physical experiment. In many ways, especially considering the historical context in which it was built (the 1920s), Sunnyside was the most idealistic and radical new town envisioned in twentieth-century America. Sunnyside, rather than a real alternative city, was never much more than a vision; as Stein put it, "Time and place and the so-called economic cycle moved the ultimate reality of our dreams."[15]

The heart of the dream was the creation of a truly diverse community in which democratic participation and civic life might flourish cooperatively. To this end, Stein formed a development corporation which was to supply the place and equipment for community gathering and activity. Tenants and house owners were to have an equal voice in community undertakings. It appears that Sunnyside residents took the encouragement of community voice too seriously. During the Depression, when faced with the loss of their homes, many went on strike against the City Housing Corporation, fighting for postponement or decrease in mortgage payments. Such a conflict between the supposedly benevolent planners and outraged residents made it obvious that it was dangerous to allow citizens to be both borrowers and lenders. Stein stated, "Constructive development of community life ended."[16] Sunnyside, however, must be considered a physical success since it continues to be a viable and visually attractive community.

After Sunnyside, the overwhelming majority of new towns built in America revolved around physical design. The driving force between new towns became Stein's "Radburn idea": building a safe suburb in a beautiful setting restricting automobiles to designated areas. Radburn was built in New Jersey in 1930. All the principal features of garden cities were eliminated before the construction of the town began; there was not an adequate portion of land to provide a greenbelt, the provision of decent homes for low-income workers was an impossibility, and no industry was planned.[17]

In fact, Radburn corresponds with Howard's theories only in its preoccupation for security, order, and design. In this case, the effectuation of the Radburn idea consisted of (1) super blocks instead of narrow, rectangular blocks; (2) specialized roads built for one use instead of all uses; (3) complete separation of pedestrian and automobile; (4) houses turned around with service entrances fronting access roads; and (5) parks, not town centers, as backbones of the neighborhood. Although this design was strikingly different from the gridiron pattern of sprawl characteristic of most American suburbs, Radburn was still nothing more than a suburb.[18]

The Radburn idea was an experiment in controlled design, a design specifically meant to cope with the automobile, not to provide an alternative city. Its main purpose was to provide order and security for the citizenry. The only social idea in the Radburn concept is the desire for order. The principles of its design have since been incorporated in most American new towns, in addition to many suburbs, and the original social basis of the garden city has been largely forgotten. Edward Eichler summarized the result:

> While a British new town is a separate physical entity, where people are intended to, and do, spend most of their daily lives, the American new community is merely a different way of organizing private development at the urban fringe of a metropolis. . . . Compared to suburban development of the last twenty years, new communities will offer a greater variety and probably a higher quality of recreational facilities such as lakes, parks, and golf courses, and they were set aside with more space. Otherwise, there has not been, and in my judgment will not be

much about the new community to differentiate them from suburbia as we know it.[19]

President Roosevelt during the 1930 Depression proposed "greenbelt towns as a reform measure to provide useful work to men on unemployment relief, demonstrate the soundness of certain garden-city principles, and provide low-rent housing." These aims were widely perceived as dangerous and socialistic, and Congress reluctantly provided for only three new towns: Green Belt, Maryland (outside Washington, D.C., and largely a response to the embarrasing Hooversville in the nation's capital); Greendale, Wisconsin (seven miles from Milwaukee); and Green Hills, Ohio (five miles from Cincinnati). Situated close to major metropolitan areas, these new towns became suburban communities from the start. Their central aim was the provision of housing. They were not conceived as self-contained cities or tools for a more desirable population pattern. They were not integrated with agriculture. Instead their green spaces were parks or vacant land. Yet even with their very limited social-aims, they were seen by many as a dangerous activity. The federal government's role as landowner and planner of greenbelt towns was resented by localities and speculators who feared a trend toward socialistic control and development. Furthermore, the greenbelt towns were seen as welfare enterprises, even though they aided the blue-collar worker rather than the unskilled poor. By the end of World War II, greenbelt towns had few supporters within or outside the Truman Administration and, accordingly, Congress voted in 1949 to sell them to private enterprise. Green Belt, Maryland, for instance, was carved up and sold to private developers. Postwar freeways had sliced the town into several sections, enabling residents to reach their downtown Washington jobs faster and erasing the community's physical integrity.[20]

In the early 1960s President Johnson was proclaiming that it was the federal government's responsibility to ensure that every American should have a decent home and that "in the next forty years we must rebuild the entire urban United States." The call for rebuilding America brought large corporations into real estate attempting to use their large capital to supply standardized housing. Their entrance into the housing market renewed discussions about new towns for America.

The Failure of Recent American New Towns

The 1960s saw the rebirth of the new town concept sponsored by the federal government. President Johnson supported federal assistance to new planned communities; however, legislation to achieve these ends, introduced by his administration in 1964, 1965, and 1966, met with opposition, or at least reservation, from a number of interest groups.[21]

The National League of Cities, the United States Conference of Mayors, and the National Association of Housing and Redevelopment Officials (NAHRO) expressed the view that any program to encourage new communities should be based upon a clearly defined national urban growth policy. In 1965 Ira S. Robbins of NAHRO told the Senate:

> It should be borne in mind that the 1946 new town legislation for Great Britain came as the culmination in the work of at least three major study commissions that had been at work on English land policy since 1918. . . . We don't think we need thirty-eight years to evolve a land-use plan for the United States; we do incline to the view that a year or two of serious work on the question of philosophy and procedure is basic.[22]

The Housing and Urban Development Act of 1968 was the first significant legislation to contain provisions for assistance to the new community concept. The passage of the act had engendered a debate wherein urban-oriented lobbies objected to the use of funds which would divert resources from the central city. It was, however, the consensus of both supporters and opponents of the bill that further study, including a review of European new towns, would be in order.

In 1968, in preparation for the implementation of the new community sections, a National Committee on Urban Growth Policy was formed. This group consisted of federal, state, and local officials, bankers, and urban affairs students. The group reviewed the latest statistics on American growth trends and organized a tour of several western European nations to study their growth policies in new towns.

This group issued a report entitled *The New City*. The report was critical of the failure of the U.S. government to formulate population growth and population distribution goals. After reviewing the European approach, the study concluded that population distribution and new town growth would and should require active federal involvement.[23]

In 1970 Congress, responding in large part to *The New City*, passed new communities legislation to be run by a community development corporation. This corporation was within the Department of Housing and Urban Development (HUD) and was to administer the new town program. The corporation was to examine, review, and coordinate policies on the growth and development of new towns. Title 7 of the 1970 legislation attempts to encourage private developers and local public agencies to build balanced, well-planned communities, with limited intrusion by the federal government and minimum impact on the federal budget. It provided what Congress considered to be a coherent, integrated package of quarantees on the direct loan and grant assistance aimed at new community development. The advocates of the 1970 legislation believed that there is a means by which more livable, less wasteful communities can be built with fewer adverse impacts on the environment, particularly when compared to suburban sprawl. One aspect of the new towns concept was a physical dimension consideration: the orderly growth of well-planned residential neighborhoods containing shopping centers, schools, and recreational facilities easily accessible to all residents, with the opportunity for jobs close at hand. The final draft of the bill, however, also had social and economic dimensions. The authors of the bill saw the new community as a place where people of all incomes and races could find an opportunity for better lives, free of the segregation precedence in many existing cities and suburbs.

The national goals of the New Community Statute—title 7 of the Housing and Urban Development Act of 1970—are:

1. Provide balanced, orderly growth: a central goal of new town development in the United States and abroad is a more workable alternative to the unplanned, haphazard growth that has been so much a part of the world scene of the past fifty years.
2. Encourage innovation: this relates to the potential of new communities for serving as laboratories for improving city development techniques.
3. Provide a total community setting for low- and moderate-income housing: due to public assistance to the new communities, it would be possible to have a broader economic and social range of Americans in privately sponsored new communities.
4. Increase choice for minorities.
5. Provide for citizen participation in adequate new community government.
6. Improve welfare of surrounding area.
7. Implement growth policy objectives: Congress intended the program to be used in both rural and center-city areas to "improve general and economic conditions in established communities so as to help reverse migration from existing cities or rural areas."[24]

The development of these new towns, through a heavy hand of government sponsorship, review, inspection, and monitoring, can be called nothing less than an unmitigated disaster. Thirteen new towns have been developed under title 7 of the 1970 Housing Act. Only 18,000 persons, or 1 to 3 percent of the total originally projected, inhabit the new towns.[25]

The admixture of governmental organization, direction, and monitoring with private development portends conflict. The real estate expert is usually an independent entrepreneur. Unlike an engineer, he does not fit into a mold or subordinate himself well to the goals of governmental intervention. Guidance from a bureaucrat is a constant irritant. When a middle-management bureaucrat calls the plays for a successful entrepreneur, the arrangement simply fails to take into account human dynamics in the form of jealousy, one-upmanship, and scrupulous rule enforcement by the individual in power. The record of such attempted combinations of governmental and entrepreneurial business is one of dissonance and conflict.

It should also be pointed out that the real estate industry is unique in the sense that it does not have a long economical production planning which allows for regulated growth. Market demand, construction interest, and permanent mortgage rates are extremely elastic and require an immediate market response. The assumptions that large industrial firms can make when contracting with government simply do not apply to real estate development. In other words, close governmental supervision of a large military order is much different than governmental supervision of a new city. The techniques are radically different and this phenomenon was poorly understood.

The review of actual statistics of the new towns is most illuminating. The following new towns are outlined: Cedar Riverside, Minnesota (table 6-1); Flower Mound, Texas (table 6-2); Harbison, South Carolina (table 6-3); Jonathan, Minnesota (table 6-4); Maumelle, Arkansas (table 6-5); Newfields, Ohio (table 6-6); Park Forest South, Illinois (table 6-7); Riverton, New York (table 6-8); St. Charles, Maryland (table 6-9); Shenandoah, Georgia (table 6-10); Soul City, North Carolina (table 6-11); Woodlands, Texas (table 6-12); and Gananda, New York (table 6-13).

To determine what went wrong, HUD contracted with the well-known management consulting firm Booz-Allen to review the program and render an evaluation report. The results of the Booz-Allen report were summarized in a white paper issued by New Communities Administration in 1976 which stated:

Table 6-1
Cedar Riverside, Minnesota

Statistics	
Location	Near the central business district, Minneapolis, Minnesota.
Total guarantee commitment	$24 million; June 1971.
Guarantees issued	Development: $24 million in debenture proceeds were expended for land acquisition, interest, and carrying costs, and administration. There has been no land development.
Population	2,800 (most preexisting jobs), 1,500 (most preexisting status).
Status	All development is enjoined as a result of an environmental lawsuit. Proceeds of title 7 debentures have been spent. HUD requested that the residents in the city agree by June 1977 on a plan for future development. Such a plan may be carried out by a public developer assisted by grants.

Source: *New Communities: Problems and Potentials,* U.S. Department of Housing and Urban Development, New Communities Administration, December 1976.

Table 6-2
Flower Mound, Texas

Statistics	
Location	Denton, Texas, 22 miles northwest of Dallas.
Total guarantee commitment	$18 million, December 1970.
Development status	Physical development began in late 1972, and stopped in June 1975.
Population	325.
Jobs	25.
Dwelling units	115.
Cost per resident	$60,000.[a]
Cost per job	$700,000.[a]
Cost per dwelling unit	$150,000.[a]

Source: *New Communities: Problems and Potentials*, U.S. Department of Housing and Urban Development, New Communities Administration, December 1976.

[a]These figures represent per unit cost.

Table 6-3
Harbison, South Carolina

Statistics	
Location	8 miles northwest of Columbia.
Total guarantee commitment	$13 million.
Development status	Physical development began in 1975; Harbison opened to public in 1976.
Population	50.
Jobs	50.
Dwelling units	55.
Cost per resident	$250,000.[a]
Cost per job	$110,000.[a]
Cost per unit	$200,000.[a]

Source: *New Communities: Problems and Potentials*, U.S. Department of Housing and Urban Development, New Communities Administration, December 1976.

[a]These figures represent per unit cost.

Table 6-4
Jonathan, Minnesota

Statistics	
Location	Chaska, Minnesota, 25 miles southwest of Minneapolis.
Total guarantee commitment	$21 million, February 1970.
Status	HUD is in process of acquiring Jonathan and attracting a new developer. The developer has not undertaken active development since late 1974.
Population	2,500.
Jobs	1,500.
Dwelling units	836.
Cost per resident	$8,400.[a]
Cost per job	$14,000.[a]
Cost per dwelling unit	$25,000.[a]

Source: *New Communities: Problems and Potentials*, U.S. Department of Housing and Urban Development, New Communities Administration, December 1976.

[a]These figures represent per unit cost.

Table 6-5
Maumelle, Arkansas

Statistics	
Location	Pulaski County, 12 miles northwest of Little Rock.
Total guarantee commitment	$25 million, February 1975.
Population	140.
Jobs	45.
Dwelling units	65.
Cost per resident	$178,500.[a]
Cost per job	$555,000.[a]
Cost per dwelling unit	$385,000.[a]

Source: *New Communities: Problems and Potentials*, U.S. Department of Housing and Urban Development, New Communities Administration, December 1976.

[a]These figures represent per unit cost.

Table 6-6
Newfields, Ohio

Statistics	
Location	Trottwood, Ohio; 7 miles northwest of Dayton.
Total guarantee commitment	$32 million, October 1973.
Development status	Development began in late 1973, and stopped in 1976.
Population	122.
Jobs	50.
Dwelling units	59 built.
Cost per resident	$262,000.[a]
Cost per job	$640,000.[a]
Cost per dwelling unit	$542,000.[a]

Source: *New Communities: Problems and Potentials*, U.S. Department of Housing and Urban Development, New Communities Administration, December 1976.

[a]These figures represent per unit cost.

Table 6-7
Park Forest South, Illinois

Statistics	
Location	Village of Park Forest South, 30 miles south of Chicago.
Total guarantee commitment	$30 million, June 1970.
Development status	Physical development began in spring of 1971, and stopped in September 1974. HUD is in process of acquiring from original developer.
Population	5,800.
Jobs	1,800.
Dwelling units	2,270.
Cost per resident	$5,000.[a]
Cost per job	$16,700.[a]
Cost per dwelling unit	$13,200.[a]

Source: *New Communities: Problems and Potentials*, U.S. Department of Housing and Urban Development, New Communities Administration, December 1976.

[a]These figures represent per unit cost.

Table 6-8
Riverton, New York

Statistics	
Location	Monroe County, 10 miles south of Rochester.
Total guarantee commitment	$21 million.
Development status	Development started in 1972, halted in 1975. HUD is negotiating to acquire Riverton.
Population	875.
Jobs	12.
Dwelling units	312 occupied.
Cost per resident	$24,000.[a]
Cost per job	$1,750,000.[a]
Cost per dwelling unit	$67,700.[a]

Source: *New Communities: Problems and Potentials*, U.S. Department of Housing and Urban Development, New Communities Administration, December 1976.

[a]These figures represent per unit cost.

Table 6-9
St. Charles, Maryland

Statistics	
Location	Charles County, Maryland, 25 miles southeast of Washington, D.C.
Total guarantee commitment	$38 million.
Development status	Development continuing.
Population	9,000.
Jobs	250.
Dwelling units	2,500.
Cost per resident	$4,200.[a]
Cost per job	$152,000.[a]
Cost per dwelling unit	$15,200.[a]

Source: *New Communities: Problems and Potentials*, U.S. Department of Housing and Urban Development, New Communities Administration, December 1976.

[a]These figures represent per unit cost.

Table 6-10
Shenandoah, Georgia

Statistics	
Location	Kawetta County, 35 miles southwest of Atlanta.
Total guarantee commitment	$25 million, March 1974.
Development status	Development continuing.
Population	7.
Jobs	30.
Dwelling units	18.
Cost per resident	$3,571,000.[a]
Cost per job	$833,000.[a]
Cost per dwelling unit	$1,389,000.[a]

Source: *New Communities: Problems and Potentials*, U.S. Department of Housing and Urban Development, New Communities Administration, December 1976.

[a]These figures represent per unit cost.

Table 6-11
Soul City, North Carolina

Statistics	
Location	Warren County, North Carolina, 45 miles north of Raleigh and Durham, near the Virginia border.
Total guarantee commitment	$10 million.
Population	55.
Jobs	116.
Dwelling units	5 model homes.
Cost per resident	$182,000.[a]
Cost per job	$86,000.[a]
Cost per dwelling unit	$2,000,000.[a]

Source: *New Communities: Problems and Potentials*, U.S. Department of Housing and Urban Development, New Communities Administration, December 1976.

[a]These figures represent per unit cost.

Table 6-12
Woodlands, Texas

Statistics	
Location	Montgomery County, 35 miles north of Houston.
Total guarantee commitment	$50 million, September 1972.
Population	2,500.
Jobs	1,200.
Dwelling units	825.
Cost per resident	$20,000.[a]
Cost per job	$41,700.[a]
Cost per dwelling unit	$60,000.[a]

Source: *New Communities: Problems and Potentials*, U.S. Department of Housing and Urban Development, New Communities Administration, December 1976.

[a]These figures represent per unit cost.

Table 6-13
Gananda, New York

Statistics	
Location	Wayne County, 12 miles east of Rochester.
Total guarantee commitment	$22,000,000.
Development status	Physical development began in late 1973; no development has occurred since October 1974.
Population	0.
Jobs	40 (school and sewer plant).
Dwelling units	3 model homes.
Cost per job	$550,000.[a]
Cost per dwelling unit	$7,333,000.[a]

Source: *New Communities: Problems and Potentials*, U.S. Department of Housing and Urban Development, New Communities Administration, December 1976.

[a]These figures represent per unit cost.

Mutual trust and respect were lacking in the HUD-developer relationship, eroded by the rapid manifestation of the mistakes made in the
approval process and by poor management.

The lack of continuity and the death of skills in large-scale development often led HUD to exhibit indecision and inflexibility. Partly
for this reason, negotiations between HUD and the developer took
far more time than is tolerable in the real estate industry.[26]

Booz-Allen concluded in their report that major factors affecting the
disaster of the title 7 program are traceable to the two following major defects
inherent in the statutory administrative design of the program:

First, the basic financing mechanism used to date under title 7—use of
the traditional compound interest-bearing debt for private acquisition
control of large amounts of land for the construction of front-end
facilities and infrastructure for the long-term development projects
is infeasible.

Second, government at all levels failed to use the new town development as a high priority tool for controlling and channeling urban
growth.[27]

Booz-Allen further reported that while the 1973-1975 economic recession
greatly exacerbated the program's difficulties, these difficulties would have
occurred in any event because of the program's basic flaws.[28]

As a consequence of the use of an interest-bearing instrument (a euphem-
ism for a loan instead of a gift), the following results occurred:

1. The developer made early commitments for land acquisition, resulting in
    heavy and inflexible front-end debt service and carrying costs.
2. HUD required unrealistically low-equity investments for projects receiving
    guarantees.
3. Developers did not receive federal grants of the types and amounts neces-
    sary to offset the front-end and carrying costs associated with a new town.
    This is in conjunction with the administration by HUD in a reactive or
    passive way.[29]

The private sector—federal government partnership in real estate has inherent defects. The normal developer's risk, that is, the fluctuation of construction
interest and market demand on a single building over a short period of time,
is multiplied many times by multiple buildings extensive road and underground
improvements, and other necessary municipal investments. An additional
element of risk is an instinctive distrust that appears to develop between the
government and the developer. Governmental regulations, cost certifications,
and red tape conflict with the developer's profit motive.

The consultants recommended that Congress should provide most if not all of the funds in any new community legislation. In other words, the only alternative is for the federal government to be a developer. The epilogue of the 1976 white paper states:

> Any revised federal assistance must reflect an acceptance that the debtor-creditor relationship traditional in the self-supporting profitable private business enterprises are not appropriate to long-term community scale development. Federal investment in new towns needs to be justified on the same basis as other federal investments in existing urban settlements: efficient commitment of public resources to achieve desirable public ends.[39]

(Booz-Allen's use of the term *investments* is a misnomer. Investment should be termed *grant*. The concept of the federal government using grants for the building and supervising of new towns is contrary to traditional economic principles and tenets of our free enterprise system and should be rejected.)

In January 1975, HUD imposed a moratorium on title 7 applications in order to devote its available resources to the existing projects. Then in 1976, HUD decided to acquire seven of the thirteen new communities from their original developers and concluded that two of the seven (Gananda, New York, and Newfields, Ohio) lacked any potential for new town development. HUD decided to recapitalize the remaining six projects. HUD recognized that events had converted its lender-grantor position to that of an equity investor, and even with that equity position many projects were precarious at best.[31]

In 1979 HUD finally gave up on the new towns under title 7. The ten-year-old New Communities Corporation will be dissolved by January 1981. These decisions came after $294 million in title 7 loan guarantees and $71.9 million in grants were in default. William J. White, director of the program, stated: "The New Communities history is a sad, painful and expensive one. What was done was done badly."[32]

The French Experience

The French program evolved between 1958 and 1965, and in 1965 formal planning was begun. The French effort was originally a program to manage the growth of the Paris region. This led to the first development of the five new towns in the Paris region, starting in 1968, and the first housing was under construction in 1970. Since then the program has been expanded to include projects near four other cities whose populations are each over 1 million. The program's primary objective now is to manage growth in the major urban areas by creating alternative growth centers 10 to 50 kilometers (about 6 to 30 miles) outside the central city of Paris.[33]

The Soviet Experience

The Soviet experience since the 1917 revolution has focused on limiting the growth of their large cities, rather than specifically creating new towns. This negative approach of limiting the growth of large cities has had an inconsistent history. The pure Marxist ideology has always had an urban bias. Marx himself used the phrase "idiocy of rural life."[34]

Communists have long held a superior air on the subject of master planning for the city. They have alleged that a master plan cannot be implemented within the framework of privately owned land. Soviet planners contend that the lack of an economic plan, private ownership of the land, and competition, all lead to disordered, uncontrolled development of the great capitalist urban areas.[35]

They maintain that only under the conditions of centralized economic planning and fully directed placing of industrial forces can the harmonious development of new social and spatial forms of settlement take place. There is no disagreement among Soviet city planners that growth of industrialization is the basic city-forming factor. The Soviets allege that failure of economic planning in the capitalist system leads to complex and complicated agglomerations, which most sharply manifest the crisis of bourgeois city planning.

Their goal is to build and encourage the vigorous life of a well-serviced and healthy city. The population must be limited; and the way to limit urban population growth is to plan carefully by directing the location and expansion of industries. Closely tied to placement of industry is the principle of proportional distribution of industry and population over the entire country, with the goal of abolishing the essential differences between town and country.

While the Soviets have been successful in abolishing private property, their performance in limitation of urban population has been less than successful. The abolition of private property began in 1918. On August 20, 1918, the cornerstone of Soviet housing policy was laid with the ratification of the decree of abolishing private ownership of urban real estate. On January 1, 1921, all rents were abolished.[36]

Under the new economic policy, rent was reestablished on June 4, 1926, and an all-union rent law was adopted. The rent rates, however, were set so low that rent revenue could not possibly cover building repairs and maintenance.[37]

It is important to note the level of apartment rent in the USSR since the issuance of the 1926 law. Rent averages about 4 to 5 percent of the family's income and covers only about 40 percent of the operational and repair costs of the housing fund.[38] The remainder of the expenditures is subsidized by government tax revenues. This tremendous subsidization results in a very low take-home pay by Soviet wage earners.

Soviet commentators are quick to point out, however, that in capitalist countries, where housing is a source of profit, rent accounts for 25 to 30 percent of the working-family's income. Hence, the rent policy in the Soviet Union is put forward as another example of that society's humanism.

To control its urbanization process, the Communist Party, as early as 1931, approved the resolution forbidding the construction of new industrial enterprises in Moscow and Leningrad as of 1932. The party declared, "that it was inexpedient to have agglomerations of huge numbers of enterprises in big urban centers."[39]

In 1970 a conference was called to discuss why the concept of population limitation was not working in the Soviet Union. During the fifty years after the revolution, the USSR is almost as urban as the United States, and in fact 40 million people have left the countryside for the city.[40] It is a fact that economic ministries of the politburo desire to take the most economical and easiest route in developing new industry. This results in large towns continuing to build industrial plants. It is often easier to build a new enterprise in a large city with highly developed transportation, electrical, and water systems. The consequences of this fact usually spell disaster for neatly researched plans for city development. It thus appears that barriers to growth are not the answer.

Conclusion

The picture of a bulldozer stripping a distant meadow for a main street of a new town is ludicrous. New towns in America are unnecessary. Starting from scratch without any established churches, businesses, or schools is imprudent. Why overlook the matrix, the roots, and the foundation of thousands of small towns?

It is undisputed that carrying costs of front-end investments in the form of streets, utilities, and municipal buildings have been identified as a chief cause of the new town defaults. While an architect may enjoy a free hand in designing an entire city, a more sensible economic approach would be to use a small town as a nucleus. An entirely new town looks too new. It appears artificial. A mixture of old and new buildings with their unique styling is more esthetically pleasing. Such a mixture reflects what is integral to nature, birth, deterioration, and regeneration.

An entirely new town would be financially viable only if it were totally subsidized or built by the federal government. This concept is fraught with difficulties in our existing society. The federal government's record as landowner and planner of towns is one of failure. Their intrusion in this field is resented by localities and home builders. The British approach, with its strong hand of central authority for the building of new towns, will not work in America.

American Dispersal Philosophers

All well-governed cities have limited populations.—Aristotle

Mumford, Wright, and Gutkind

Lewis Mumford, historian and urban scholar, is the best known of twentieth-century American proponents of dispersion. Although Mumford never drew up a specific plan for city building or population dispersal, his thinking on the need for new urban forms has been widely influential.

For Mumford, the key to the good city was the small-scale environment. In *The Urban Prospect*, he wrote: "We shall never succeed in dealing effectively with the complex problems of large units and differentiated groups unless at the same time we rebuild and revitalize the small unit. . . . If we are to recapture the initiative from our machine-centered civilization, we must establish a life-centered environment from the moment of birth."[1]

Like Howard, Mumford believed in stability and planned order, and a balance between congestion and sprawl in regional systems that would link a network of cities set in a midst of publicly protected open spaces permanently dedicated to agriculture and recreation. But Mumford's goals and emphasis are very different from those of Howard's. For Mumford, population dispersal was far from an end in itself; it was a means of recapturing old urban values and the means of reorienting the ideals of the whole civilization: a means toward personal fulfillment. Howard's garden city may be seen as an orderly means of coping with the ills of technology; Mumford's ideas, though never articulated as a design, were a means of battling the economic and value systems of which the ills of technology were only a part. Because he recoiled from what he saw as the congestion and disorder of the contemporary city, Mumford is sometimes criticized as a celebrator of the simple rural life. In fact, Mumford believed that urban values—variety, multiformity, social complexity, and concentration—were the essence of human civilization. He believed that these values were best realized on a small scale, as they were in the Greek polis or medieval commune.

While a certain rural nostalgia may permeate some of Mumford's concepts, most of them seek to recreate the lost vitality of the metropolis by establishing cities on a smaller scale or by providing means of self-government and control. This is in accord with progressive thinkers. There was, however, an American school of thought which did idealize the simple rural existence and which does honestly seek to destroy the city. Thomas Jefferson, for example, expressed mistrust and hostility toward urban life, which he suspected would destroy the nation of independent farmers he knew.[2] In the twentieth century, this concept has been expressed by architect Frank Lloyd Wright. Because Wright is often categorically lumped with American decentralists, his views should be further examined to differentiate them from those of Mumford and others.

Wright saw cities as temporary necessities, essentially antihuman entities which were built to provide human contact before the advent of swift communication and transportation. He thought technology could liberate people from enslavement to the city and postulated a clearly utilitarian city that would meet minimal economic needs and leave people free to live elsewhere.

Wright railed against centralization. He stated: "The strength of will and courage of our original pioneers was a native forerunner of this type of domination we now see building its own mortal monuments—the skyscrapers and the cemeteries that are the 'great' cities. They mark the end of an epoch. The industrial revolution. . . . Pioneering now lies along this new frontier: decentralization."[3]

Wright's conception of decentralization envisioned decentralized factories and farms.

> Light, strong houses and workplaces will be built out of the nature of the ground into sunlight. Factory workers will live on acre home units within walking distance or a short right-of-way from the future factories. Factories, beautiful, smokeless and noiseless. No longer will the farmer envy the urban dweller his mechanical improvements while the latter in turn covets the farmer's green pastures.

> Each factory and farm would be within a ten-mile radius of a vast and variegated wayside market, so that each can serve the other simply and effectively and both can serve that other portion of the population which lives and works in the neighborhood of that market. No longer will any need exist for futile racing to a common center and racing back again, crucifying life just to keep things piled up "big."[4]

The conditions which Wright felt were natural to people were pure dispersal: spread out, very-low-density settlements in which each family would occupy a large and isolated space, hopefully doing its own subsistence farming. This broad-acre city of less than 800 families would occupy a site as large as New York's Central Park.[5] No urban-living container would exist at all. Mumford comments: "This fantasy of Wright's was based both on his wholesome appreciation of the hygienic and dynastic values of rural life and his contempt for the many-sided corporate and institutional life of the city."[6] In fact, Wright's ideal of the self-sufficient rural household and low-density settlement has been debased, but still expressed, in the isolated and wealthy homes of exurbia.

Victor Gruen is also a renowned advocate of a new urban pattern. In *The Heart of Our Cities*, Gruen attempted to revitalize humane civic living: a renaissance of compactness, intense and creative public life, diverse population, and intermingling of activities. To accomplish this, he proposed to break down the metropolis into cells of human scale. To encourage a sense of place, control, and belonging, and to provide access to the best of cultural and economic opportunity, this scheme is very similar to Howard's design, though Gruen assumed an overall metropolitan area at ten times that of Howard's population, or 300,000. Gruen envisioned the metropolitan center as the most densely built-up and most intensively utilized land area, containing universities and cultural facilities. Each cell is separated from the others by greenbelts. High-speed public transportation is integrated with the use of the private automobile. Industry is segregated into special zones.[7]

Gruen's plan is largely one of design, leaving intact the walls of economic structure and technology of contemporary society. He seeks to reverse certain trends: toward suburban scatterization, increased use of the automobile, and decentralization of urban function. He assumes that such trends can be reversed by educating humane and sophisticated planners, who will presumably realize the benefits of pedestrian malls and monorails. His scheme is essentially stripped of all socialistic elements. Even though he advocates the breakup of the metropolis into small manageable cells, it is highly questionable whether Gruen planned for true dispersal. The notion of small units within large ones is advocated by a wide range of people, many of whom have no interest in dispersal. For example, Mitchell Gordon states that effective functioning of large cities requires a breakdown into "total communities of manageable size."[8] He asserts that powerful, metropolitanwide government must be created, but it must rule over a collection of small units interspersed with green. By and large, this view is based on a functional analysis, and its goal is the efficient and orderly functioning of the large cities.

E.A. Gutkind, on the other hand, wanted to eliminate the role of the city as an all-absorbing center.[9] He desired to establish a "centerless region of numerous small communities, joined together in a dense social and economic structure." As initial means to this, he advised an end to slum rebuilding in central cities; an evacuation of commercial, cultural, and industrial institutions from central cities; and the gradual transformation of the older urban landscape into a continuous park system. In contrast to Howard and Gruen, Gutkind believed that physical dispersal must be accompanied by cultural dispersal, not simply placed near old cultural centers.

Gutkind's proposal is reminiscent of others in its call for urban-rural integration, effective participatory planning, small-scale communities, and regional systems. However, it has a unique flavor of futurism. Gutkind seeks to create a system which is uniquely adapted to the possibilities of the technological age. His principal thesis is the notion of a centerless region as the next phase in the evolution of the environmental structure. Far from regretting the loss of the flourishing city, he feels that cities belong to a bygone era and can never be adapted to the contemporary context. He believes that an intellectual revolution is taking place which will reduce our present metropolitan form into a museum piece.

The great advantage of the technological age, as Gutkind sees it, is mobility—near-simultaneity in space and time. Rather than being limited to a single place and to an extent defined by that place, each human being can be his own mobile center. Rather than depend on a metropolis for economic opportunity and cultural stimulation, people will find these elements in their own communities; and they will have easy access to many other equally important communities. Living space will be greatly expanded. Small communities, instead of creating a simple and smaller environment as in Gruen's proposal, will eliminate parochialism and will create a wider scale of living than any known before. Life will no longer be focused on a small place but on an entire region, in which no part is predominant.

Gutkind thus locates the traditional amenities of urban living—access to excitement, culture, diversity, and personal opportunity—in a collective region rather than within an urban container. He states:

> In the new structure of settlement there may be university towns similar to those which already exist, as, for instance, Princeton, Oxford, Cambridge, but of a purer character, not spoilt by the encroachment of industries. There may be places where theater and opera performances imprint their mark on the life of the community. There may be museum towns from which traveling exhibitions are regularly sent out. There may be festival towns where special entertainments are organized. The rudiments of this dispersal do exist, and it is necessary only to evolve them further and to get rid of the notion that most of these opportunities should be concentrated in one or several big cities.[10]

Other noted dispersalists, Bookchin and Goodman, believe that social goals must be revised to achieve ecological balance.[11] They envision a change in economic structuring and use of technology, in addition to different physical design, in order to realize a new human relationship with the natural environment. One such integrated plan is offered by the editors of *The Ecologist*, in their *Blueprint for Survival*.[12] These editors feel that the ecological balance will not be obtained and endure until human beings realize a stable society, one which is not oriented toward constant growth. Such a stable society entails restraints and controls to prevent wasting of resources, encroachment on farmland, and pollution of the atmosphere. Small-scale communities are best equipped to work out these restraints in a democratic manner; whereas in a large-scale, heterogeneous, and centralized system, restraints would appear as so much outside coercion. Moreover, the editors believe that small-scale communities are the best nutrient for individuality and creativity. The central idea of *Blueprint for Survival* is that the physical design must be linked intimately with the social purpose if it is to achieve real change in societal structure.

Murray Bookchin seeks to reestablish the humanistic attributes of traditional cities in small-scale form, such as the Greek polis. Bookchin believes that only in the industrial era did the city grow so big as to lose this definition and sense of solidarity. According to Bookchin: "There is a point beyond which a city negates itself, churning up a human condition that is more atomizing and culturally and socially more desiccated than any attributed to rural life."[13]

Bookchin views the capitalist economic ethic as largely responsible for the growth in urban life. In this sense, reestablishment of the sense of community, individual importance, and urban-rural integration depend on the establishment of a small and socialistic community. He believes that social responsibility can never be nurtured in a capitalistic environment. His proposal is integrated in that it seeks to change the nature of work as well as the conventions of residential living. Rather than relying on professional and physical planning to achieve his goals, he recommends deep structural changes in the economy and the values of society. The reestablishment of urbanity, according to Bookchin, demands social change, not merely physical design.

Critics of the Dispersal Philosophers

Some critics feel that dispersal will destroy the essence of the city. William H. Whyte stated:

> Decentralize or concentrate? Most of the prescriptions for the ideal metropolis opt for decentralization. . . . This kind of decentralization would not only be a very inefficient way to accommodate growth, it would go against the grain of all the forces that give a metropolis its vitality. Rather than pursue this ill-conceived provincialism, we must look inward as well as outward, to the strengths of the metropolis and seek a much more intensive and efficient use of land already within it.[14]

The belief that large populations have a monopoly on excitement and vitality is a view held by John Eli Burchard. He writes:

> Some people are just too depressed by the details of daily urban life to accept them as a price for the high moment that the metropolis alone can provide. They propose solutions in communities of "human scale," say, of 50,000. I always find this a little amusing and also puzzling. Where are these human communities? Are Brockton and Fitchburg, Massachusetts, Cumberland and Hagerstown, Maryland, more human than Rome or Paris—or for that matter, really, New York or Chicago? Let me be quite dogmatic about this. A city of 50,000 can manage a good, safe, comfortable, unexciting life for all its citizens. If this is all anybody wants, we can have it; and there is no sense today in anything bigger. For most, if not all, of the technical and economic reasons for the big city have disappeared.[15]

Burchard feels that small-scale urban centers will be necessarily monotone and boring, lacking in such amenities as symphony orchestras, important museums, excellent theater, sophisticated newspapers, and the like.

In contemporary American society, it is certainly true that cultural dynamism is centered in the biggest cities. However, this is the result of our economic structure which makes the arts a segment of private enterprise. Supported only to a minimum extent by public funds, the arts actually gravitate to areas providing the largest and most compact market. That is, they flourish in the centers of the largest metropolises. If population were effectively dispersed into smaller centers, the arts would presumably disperse also. There is simply no evidence that people who live in large cities are inherently more appreciative of the arts than people who live in small cities. Indeed, Otis Dudley Duncan found that there is a negative correlation between city size and per capita use of cultural facilities, such as museums and libraries. Even though larger cities have larger libraries, the circulation of library books per capita markedly decreases with size of city.[16] The extent to which culture can flourish in small centers is very much dependent on public attitudes. Duncan also estimates that the requisite population base for a library of desirable minimal professional standards is 50,000 to 75,000; for an art museum, 100,000.[17] Moreover, there is no reason why smaller cities cannot band together for specific purposes, such as for cultural advantages presently enjoyed by large populations.

Conclusion

Mumford, Gutkind, Wright, and Gruen all agree that there is an acute need for population dispersal. Each offers a unique method to achieve a better city. Mumford envisions a new civilized city. He views the atmosphere of the cosmopolitan cities of the nineteenth century as a paradigm of the habitat for civilized man. Gudkind, a true futurist, throws centralism to the wind and strikes out in a new dimension of total dispersal. Planners Wright and Gruen fall back on physical layouts.

A common thread among the dispersalists is the questioning of the society and a value system based on constant growth. The overconcentration of population is the by-product of a consumption-oriented society. After review of the dispersalists' plans, the question remains whether the pressure for growth can be alleviated in a capitalistic system. Bookchin directly confronts the question and contends that the reestablishment of a sense of community is incompatible with the capitalistic system. He sees large concentrations as a direct result of the capitalistic ethic.

Change to a socialistic or planned economy is not necessary for a change in our value system. The constant quest for more things is a mental state rather than the direct result of an economic system. The willingness to put up with disamenities of a large city to buy a few more goods is changing. Spontaneous movement to a nonmetropolitan area and the overwhelming desire of urban residents to move to smaller cities are early indicators that the value system can and does change in a capitalistic society.

Our Urban Heritage

The environment men create through their wants becomes a mirror that reflects their civilization; more importantly, it also constitutes a book in which is written the formula of life that they communicate to others and transmit to succeeding generations. Characteristics of the environment are therefore of importance not only because they affect the comfort and quality of present-day life, but even more because they condition the development of young people and thereby of society.—René Dubos

Cities have existed in a variety of forms for 5,000 years. The three most significant historical stages in the maturation of the city are the ancient, the polis, and the renaissance city.

Ancient City

The first cities were built to provide security. A community of persons and possessions was surrounded by a wall which provided protection from war and other intrusions by hostile forces. As the inside-the-wall dwellers became more secure, constant vigil for survival became less and less necessary. This security released residents and allowed them freedom of time to develop more specialized commerce, organize religion, and create structures to govern and regulate interpersonal relationships. In the ancient cities, religion played a dominant role as shown by the temples, domes, and squares dedicated to the city's deities. The religious center was often supplemented by a central marketplace. Capital was accumulated by rulers and businessmen, and the accouterments of arts, sciences, and sports evolved.

Adam Smith observed that "order and good government and along with them the liberty and security of individuals, were in this manner established in cities at a time when the occupiers of land and the country were exposed to every sort of violence."[1]

Greek Polis

The Greek polis, or city-state, emerged in the fifth century B.C. These city-states were radically different from the ancient cities. Unlike residents of most ancient cities, the Greeks were not subjects of an agrarian monarchy. Their equality as citizens was based on their status as landholders. The polis embodied a public participation unknown to rural dwellers. The principal activity was community life in the agora (assembly place). All policy decisions were formulated directly by a popular assembly (ecclesia) which every male citizen was expected to attend. Civic agencies were manned by citizens and reconstituted every year.

This social and governmental structure can be understood only in light of its historical setting. The polis did not develop out of economic drives or political force. It was based on the very social nature of Greek culture. To a Greek, the polis was the man, and the man the polis. To be exiled from the polis was to suffer extinction more horrifying than death. The Hellenic citizen was nourished by his community and produced science, philosophy, and literature. Although the polis contained seeds of democracy, it was a bastion of slavery and patriarchal treatment of women.[2]

The polis was small by modern standards of urbanization. Athens supported 30,000 citizens at its zenith and was the product of the deliberate philosophy that population should be limited. This size of the polis fulfilled the demand of Aristotle that the polis should have the largest number which suffices for the purpose of life and can be taken in at a single view.[3]

The Renaissance City

In the thirteenth century cities began to form as serfs attempted to escape their feudal yokes. Some cities enacted charters which granted certain political liberties. The charter often stipulated that any serf who took refuge in a city and lived there a year and a day without being recovered by his master was thereafter a citizen. "City air makes a man free" became a German proverb.[4] This freedom attracted new settlers from land to city. The cities became small trade centers and free enterprise was born and nurtured. The church played an important role, as the cathedrals that survive testify. Urban dwellers were devoted to their city, appreciated their civic virtues, and took responsibilities seriously.

The medieval city was built as a fortress. It was surrounded by walls, surmounted by towers, pierced by gates, and encircled by a moat. In the center of each city was a public square or marketplace, facing the principal church, town hall, and guild hall. The houses generally used their ground floors as workshops and upper floors as residences. Most medieval cities had a stabilized size. Arnold Toynbee explains that the size of such a city and the area of the hinterland were determined by how far a farmer could get his horse and produce into town and back home again the same night.[5]

The medieval city laid the foundation for the nation state. It weakened the control of the church and feudal lords and gave birth to self-rule. This experience of citizenship and autonomy in business prepared the way for urban political democracy. As we shall also see, it was the basis for the value system which was carried to America and has become an important part of our tradition.

A study of historical cities reveals that a city is more than a mere agglomeration of people and buildings. Every city was molded by its particular social and historical setting. Cities have had innumerable forms and adaptations to historical settings. There has not been a predictable development since the continued change in forms is as diverse as civilization itself.

The Greeks, with their particular set of values and the state of their technological art, created a unique urban system at a unique moment in history. The polis may be regarded as an exceptionally productive, refined city form. However, like every other urban system, it was molded by the historical, cultural, and technological constraints of its time. American cities do not differ from the polis because Americans have failed to study the polis. Our cities are different because they have developed from a radically different philosophy, with different technological tools at another unique time in history. Since a city is only relevant when viewed in its particular context, a meaningful universal definition of the term *city* is impossible. The fact that the Greek polis is different in virtually every aspect from a contemporary American city illustrates that the word *city* has no meaningful universal definition.

The term *urban system* is more the apt description. It is used to emphasize that each urban system is unique, belonging to a special set of historical circumstances. Further, the United States is urbanized to the extent that what we commonly call urban problems are no longer specifically associated with officially bounded cities. Our urban system is shaped by values, institutions, and structures which affect all our population, not only those who live in congested or incorporated areas.

It will thus be shown that the development of the American urban system is not based on a universal theory of urban development, but on the specific history, technology, and values of its people.

Cities of the Industrial Revolution

Our new nation was originally populated by settlers who had no idea that they were eventually to build an intensely urbanized system. They brought values of an agrarian society and bourgeois values of middle-class society of small proprietors. The new world's settlers were often fleeing from the constraints of the old feudal order. These immigrants regarded the possession of land as the path of escape from tyranny and the key to dignity, status, and individual autonomy. These values created a climate and structure in America which influenced not only the frontier but also the development and growth of our cities.

The nineteenty-century industrial revolution was the force behind the urbanization of America. It overhauled virtually all previous modes of life, giving rise to new values and new institutions. The industrial revolution also gave impetus to the growth of a new urban system which we know as the *metropolis*. The metropolis is distinguished from earlier cities by a much greater population and separated employment and residential areas, which in turn are segregated according to class and income of the residents.

The industrial revolution brought about the blossoming of the capitalistic system. Leaders of industry came to possess huge amounts of capital and embraced a value system known as laissez-faire or classic capitalism. The values and emphasis on private property by this new leadership class had far-reaching implications, molding the values of America's inhabitants.

The cities of the industrial era ceased to be reflections of individual, dynastic, or collective personalities. They became the instrument, the result, and the product of the industrial development. Americans conceived their cities as places of business. This concept was much different than prior city conceptions on the continent. The previously described polis, for example, was a collective reflection of Greek culture. In like manner, Egyptian and Chinese cities were monuments to the creation of a dynamic personality; Aztec cities reflected the glory of the individual god-king. Even feudal medieval communities were self-contained entities founded on a sense of collective personality and duty rather than created solely for the economic benefits of the individual. The beautiful cathedrals in small European cities were built as a communal effort and were reflections of a collective sense of place and duty. While there are some American communities which were built as a communal effort and reflected a collective sense of place and duty, most American cities are the product of a solely economic rationale. The growth of cities based on this economic value system started a rate of urbanization so great that theories of urban development based on the pre-1800 cities became largely irrelevant. The impact of economic urbanization on society is such that society gives way to urban institutions, urban values, and urban demands. Its effect is so dynamic that some urbanologists have called the process irreversible.[6] The forces of the industrial revolution and its economic urbanization were so powerful that the whole institutional structure has been affected as a consequence of this urban development.

The urbanization in America was not softened by the civic traditions of the European experience. In Europe, the impact of the industrial urbanization was felt through a screen of social structure and urban inheritance going back many generations, European cities contained historical structures and a tradition of city life not entirely formed by economic demands and relationships.

The contribution of a long preindustrial history to the current character of European cities prevented the complete changeover to a modern metropolis as was the American experience.

Privatism and the Urban Development

In America, private ownership of land has become synonymous with personal liberty. This association of property with individual rights and liberties was a radical change from previous societies in which land has always been regarded in some sense as a social resource.

The conception of private ownership of land as liberty, along with the laissez-faire economic system, became the central tenet of American democracy. This unique and peculiar combination of values spawned the notion that liberty is intertwined with landownership, a philosophy that is quite distinct from the European experience. This uniquely American tradition has been described as privatism.[7]

Land in America generally has been conceived as the springboard to individual wealth, the basis of individual liberty, and the just province of individual decision making. This society holds the conception that each individual can freely pursue his own interests, relying on a limited police power to protect the general public's health, safety, and welfare as in the best interest of society. As a result of these views, American land has become a personal asset rather than a social resource whom use is determined by communal decision.

The idealism of "liberty-land" has had far-reaching implications in the formation of our system. The American philosophy stresses land development and not land protection. This system is characterized by the view that each individual is free to develop the land as he personally sees fit.

Popular enthusiasm for individualistic land law resulted in early federal statutes which codified the colonial custom so that all land west of the Alleghenies would be held and descend according to fee simple.[8] Fee-simple descent is radically different from the European tradition of primogeniture, which resulted in one family owning the same land for generations. This early governmental sanction allowed American land to be freely exchanged wherein price is determined by the economic market. No hindrance has been imposed by the existence of giant tracts of land tied up in perpetual legal restrictions. The consistent public pressure for land dispersal caused the American land to be subdivided and sold to private landowners at a fantastic rate. By 1862, with the passage of the Homestead Act, a settler could receive 160 acres of surveyed land after five-years residency upon the payment of the registration fee of $26 to $34.[9]

It has been estimated that one-fourth of all congressional activity in the nineteenth century was concerned with land legislation.[10] Public support was based on the political platform of egalitarianism. The belief that any settler could gain ownership of land created a tradition that has endured. The great American public-land sales of the nineteenth century allowed virtually anyone to buy. The consequence of this federal-land-disposal policy created an extreme dispersion of decision making since each property owner considered himself autonomous in relationship to his land.

Another legacy from the federal land system of the early-nineteenth century is the federal survey system. The survey's basic unit was a township of 6 square miles subdivided into thirty-six sections. The cities and towns were based on a symmetrical grid system. This survey technique contributed permanent features to our urban landscape. The grid system usually failed to produce centered or bounded neighborhoods. There was rarely a central park or piazza as in the European experience. Thus the natural center of the federal land survey became the main street or highway strip. In addition, the open-grid pattern provided no fixed boundaries for neighborhoods, no point from which city dwellers could define their own vicinity visually and socially against the endless metropolitan complex. It is possible to enter and leave towns in metropolitan areas without recognizing the fact. The grid system was frequently followed in laying out subdivisions. Developers often measured their success in numbers of lots, each laid out on a grid of streets with little regard to topography or the lots of neighbors.

The setting of privatism with its disadvantages and advantages is the basic factor creating our urban system of today. The setting of today is based on our heritage; it was and is strongly based on the concept that private ownership of land is the chief characteristic of liberty.

The Early Urban Environment

The private ownership of American land in the rural environment allowed self-contained residential units where the landowner was able to furnish his own food, maintain his roads, and provide for garbage and sewage disposal. The effect of the industrial revolution on urban residents created the need for interdependence. However, this was not noticed immediately. The eighteenth-century city consisted of small independent proprietors. This tradition of privatism and the social economic environment of the colonial town complemented each other. It was assumed that there would be no major conflicts between private interests and public welfare. However, as urban areas became larger, denser, and more heterogeneous, the tradition of privatism actually prevented the improvement of individual life and the public environment. The nineteenth-century city was an excellent place for economic opportunity, but it was woefully unable to cope with such public problems as sanitation, fire control, safety, housing, and overall urban beauty.

The European experience, though encountering similar problems due to the industrial revolution, responded more effectively to the social crises induced by industrialization. Early reliance on public enterprise in such cities as Glasgow and Birmingham produced such exemplary services that municipal authorities in many European cities assumed responsibility for supplying water, gas, electricity, and public transportation at moderate rates.[11] Such was not the case in the American city, and early Europeans were horrified at the conditions in early urban America.

The French traveler M.L.E. Moreau de Saint-Méry described New York in 1817 while taking the evening air:

> They sit facing each other on benches put at right angles to their houses. Even if they were in favor of promenading, which they aren't, this is not commendable because pigs and cows got the idea first. Besides, no one thinks of removing the dead dogs and cats and rats from the street.[12]

Garbage and manure in the streets reached incredible levels in Boston before officials decided to act: "Since most people took public filth for granted, getting rid of it, all of a sudden, may have seemed to them nothing short of betrayal." Eventually, it was decided that a one-time cleanup should be organized. A sort of cleaning orgy instead of a regular program of garbage removal was performed. All were disappointed when the filth inevitably returned.[13]

The image of pigs and cows roaming the streets of Manhattan is amusing but the results of such lack of control were often deadly. Unsanitary conditions were prevalent throughout the nation, and every port or river town was stricken with epidemics of smallpox, cholera, and yellow fever. The yellow fever epidemic of 1793 in Philadelphia took a death toll of more than 5,000 persons in a population of about 55,000. Called "the most appalling collective disaster that had ever overtaken an American city," it easily jarred Americans into sensing the darker side of city life.[14]

After numerous epidemics causing widespread death and devastating fires which destroyed substantial cities, an awareness that individual health and property depended on general protection of life and property arose. Public health boards were created in many cities. Concern for security of property against chronic fire hazards made possible the enactment of building restrictions and encouraged the organization of fire deparments.

The barbaric conditions of the nineteenth-century city did not stem the increasing flow of new residents. American cities grew at a rate far exceeding European cities during the industrial revolution expansion. The nine largest American cities grew two to three times as fast as their European counterparts.[15]

The physical characteristics of the American city reflected the amorphous collection of traders and merchants who founded them. The focus on economic gain created the development of a region rather than a city. Having no previous history of physical or political boundaries, American cities grew in all directions, without a recognized distinction between urban and rural territory. In contrast, the bounded cities of Europe have always offered the residents a self-contained way of life, one that is separated from that of the rest of the country in profound ways. This distinctness, based on a long urban heritage, created a loyalty to the city and an overall civic consciousness.

The concepts of civic leadership in the American city were usually promulgated by the business leaders of the community. Their preoccupation was on economic growth. In historical American towns, as in many towns in America even today, the most widely representative community body was the Chamber of Commerce. Its leaders were businessmen who were more interested in low taxes and freedom from municipal control than in public services. The affairs of the city thus came to be dominated by a few powerful men, necessarily of conservative interests, who saw the duty of government to be the defense of private property.

Despite its lack of overall civic consciousness and social responsibility, the American city between 1820 and 1870 was the "zenith of our national urbanity." This urbanity was found in the "mixture of blacks and whites, along with the dense living and crowded streets in the omnipresence of all manner of businesses near the homes in every quarter."[16] This era more than any subsequent era in American urban history embodied the virtues of variety and multiformity often associated with a cosmopolitan city. However, even in this era of the early 1800s, it is difficult to apply the terms *urbanity* or *cosmopolitanism* to American cities. The distinction must be made between urbanization and citification. Americans wanted to gain the economic benefits of urbanization while continuing to resist the way of life usually associated with living in cosmopolitan European centers.

America and the Suburb

The burgeoning cities, while abundant in economic opportunities, provided undesirable living conditions. The desire to separate one's place of work from one's residence led to the development of the periphery town, known as the suburb. The suburb is a manifestation of an anticity bias long existent in American philosophy. Agrarianism, or rural independence, is an American tradition shaped by the fusion of private property with personal liberty. This philosophy has shown tangible expression in the movements of residential America. When the city dwellers were economically capable, the urbanites turned into suburbanites. The suburbanization process was in progress well before the auto age and has been going on for at least a century.

From the very early days of America, the overwhelming goal of most urban residents appears to have been to escape the city. The city has been conceived of as a necessary place for work but an unsuitable place to live. As early as 1823 advertisements in New York newspapers beckoned urbanites with the pastoral idealism of suburban living. This advertisement was published by *The New York Times* in 1823:

Situated directly opposite the Southwest part of the city, and being the nearest country retreat, and the easiest of access from the center of business that remains unoccupied, the distance not exceeding an average of 15 to 25 minutes to walk, including the passage of the river; the ground elevated and perfectly healthy at all seasons; the view of water and landscape both extensive and beautiful, as a place of residence all the advantages of the country with most of the conveniences of the city. . . . Gentlemen whose business or profession requires your daily attendance in the city cannot better, or with less expense, secure the health and comfort of their families.[17]

With the advent of streetcars in 1870, suburban living became possible for vast numbers. By 1900 more then one-half of Boston's families were isolated from the city in the suburbs.[18] Sam Warner, in his classic study of streetcar suburbs in Boston, documents the transformation of the city: "In 1850, the metropolitan region of Boston encompassed a radius of but two or three miles, population of 200,000; in 1900, the region extended over a 60-mile radius and contained a population of more than 1 million."[19]

The reasons given for suburban living are manifold. Undoubtedly the new suburbanites sought more than physical peace and serenity. They may have needed some psychological calm as a palliative to the fierce competitiveness of the American city. In a cultural atmosphere which promoted constant self-advancement and affluence, it was more secure to live in an environment of economic equals. The growth of the suburb was also due to the belief that everyday life should be primarily a value-reinforcing experience rather than primarily a value-altering one.[20] This homogeneity was provided by suburban living. The best way to ensure continued values is to isolate one's self and one's children in an environment dominated by other families and children whose social, economic, cultural, and even religious views and attitudes are approximately the same as one's own.

When considering whether the suburban experience is positive, one should not lose sight of the fact that at least half of the metropolitan population has been excepted from the suburban experience. Though the suburbs may have had an effect of relieving urban congestion, such relief was small and further thwarted by the withdrawal of capital, talent, and decent housing from the central city. The suburbs eventually came to fear and mistrust the city. The suburb had the effect of segregating the metropolitan area population by class. Although the expansion of the streetcar and other municipal services provided the rationale for annexation of the central city with the suburbs, the issue of annexation was short-lived. In Boston, for example, by 1880 none of the thirty suburbs would ever seriously consider annexation with the central city again.[21]

The suburban rush of early America cannot be regarded as an automatic response to the congestion provoked by industrialization, immigration, and economic opportunity. In Europe, for example, the move to the suburbs was a trickle compared to America. The heritage of urban living in Europe led city

residents to create new social institutions, public housing, and other new structures to cope with the new ills. The European literature was one of revolt against
the industrial city conditioned by an urban tradition, a memory of and a pride
in humane cities. In America, on the other hand, the community was not the
prize goal. Suburbanization was the form which resulted from the response that
new frontier land or open land was a solution. This pioneer belief in space and
mobility as a panacea of social ills may be traced to a frontier mentality of
the early American urbanites. This cultural and psychological background was
accentuated by a governmental policy which was heavily weighted in favor of
the home owner and the low-density development.

The move to the suburb created new urban patterns. The pattern of inner
poverty, rings of increasing affluence, and pie-shaped wedges of commercial
and industrial property stretching out from downtown can still be seen today.
This new pattern settled upon early American cities with remarkable sudden-
ness and reemphasized the economic character of the city. The Chicago School
of Urbanology, led by Robert Park, demonstrated how the people of the city
were systemized by work relationships and bound into a gigantic metropolitan
economic web.[22] Economic and ethnic bounds appear to outweigh any civic
consciousness or sense of political direction.

By the end of the nineteenth century the impact of the metropolis was
clear. The city and country in America could no longer be thought of as a
distinct and imposed environment, as the city extended enormously its spatial
area and social influence. In 1906 municipal reformer Frederick Howe wrote:
"The city has become the central figure in modern civilization and to an ever-
increasing extent, the dominant one. This rural civilization, whose making
engaged mankind since the dawn of history is passing away. The city has erased
the landmarks of an earlier society. Man has entered on an urban age."[23]

Howe was correct in recognizing the dominance of the city. However, in
America the dominant form was not the traditional European city with its
attributes of cosmopolitanism, diversity of youth, and social mixture. The
American form was a unique urban system which attempted to blend the aspects
of urban and rural existence. The American urban places are preeminently anticity, implicitly developed to reflect the basic American life-style and tradition.

The American intellectual tradition has also been largely antiurban. Jefferson, Emerson, Thoreau, Hawthorne, Melville, Poe, Henry Adams, Henry James,
Lewis Sullivan, Frank Lloyd Wright, and John Dewey have all expressed varying
degrees of hostility toward urban life in America.[24] This intellectual and literary
tradition has been coined as pastoralism by some commentators.[25] Pastoralism
has been defined as a movement toward nature, an upward expression of a
search for happiness, order, and meaning.

The actual development of the American urban system also reflected an
urge to retreat from the machine and the economically dominated city. The
effect of this suburban movement did not preserve the distinctness of city

and country but rather blended the two environments. This blending was evident by the end of the nineteenth century. Frederick Howe was sent abroad by the U.S. government to study municipal problems. When viewing his homeland from abroad, he stated:

> Our cities are what they are because we have no thought of the city as a city, of a town as a town, of the right of everybody to the rights of anybody. Our cities have been permitted to grow with no concern for the future. . . . We lack a city sense. There is nothing to awaken love, affection, interest. . . . The city has neglected the people and the people in turn have neglected the city.[26]

This pattern of rural-style living led inevitably to the metropolitanism evidenced so early in American cities. Dependent on the resources of their hinterlands and expanding rapidly into them, American cities have never been self-contained civic entities. This returns us to the thesis that our cities are the product of a unique set of American values, state of technology, and a particular stage of maturation of our society. The American urbanism is one of the innumerable forms of cities. The future would be predictable if values and technology crystallized, but since values and technology are in a constant flux, one cannot with assurance predict future urban forms.

The Growth of the City

It is better to be the head of a village than the tail of a city.—Anonymous

In 1790 when the newly formed national government initiated the first census, 95 percent of 3.9 million Americans were rural. The census further listed Philadelphia with 42,000 inhabitants and New York with 33,000. Ten years later Philadelphia's population was 70,000 and New York's was 60,000.[1]

The pre-Civil War period witnessed the formation of most of our present cities. Between 1790 and 1890, America's total population grew sixtyfold. At the beginning of the period the average married couple had eight children. Many cities doubled their population every decade between 1850 and 1900. By 1900, fifty American cities had populations in excess of 100,000.[2]

Pre-World War I Growth

The building boom of 1870 to 1920 manifested the urban growth, and the results of this dynamic era remain visible today since the bulk of the existing buildings in our central cities were built during this era. This construction was demanded by the phenomenal increase in population as shown in Chicago's growth from 300,000 in 1870 to 3 million in 1920. Milwaukee zoomed from 70,000 to 500,000 in the same era.[3] This was also a period of virtually unrestricted immigration from Europe. Between 1890 and 1920, 18.2 million immigrants arrived in the United States and accounted for 42 percent of the overall population growth in those three decades. Most immigrants settled in cities, and in 1920 fully three-quarters of foreign-born populations were urban residents.[4] For example, in 1920, 1.1 million residents of Chicago were immigrants.[5]

The underlying cause for the spectacular growth was the industrial revolution and its concomitant economy-of-scale production. The large factories located in urban centers created an unquenchable demand for blue-collar workers. Much as the ancients moved to the city for commerce, jobs, and security, the urban movement of the nineteenth century was based in large part on economic determinants. It soon became evident that jobs were more abundant in the city, and this realization provided the impetus to move for a great part of the rural populace. The attraction of the city was high-paying jobs and identification with the segment of society termed progressive. A farmer who was working twelve hours a day for $2.00 did not have to be convinced to come to Detroit when Henry Ford offered $5.00 per day. The period from 1920 to 1929 witnessed unprecedented factory growth in the city. As agrarian labor lost its value, the city drew the peasant toiler. The growth was principally due to the manpower required by the manufacturing sector. The service sector was insignificant during this early period. Industrial America learned to mass-produce, and the public began to consume at a rate never before experienced. Sewing machines, stoves, and other appliances formerly considered luxuries were becoming necessities of the day and created widespread demand.

The metropolitan areas of the turn of the century were a workers' market. This great demand in turn offered job advancement and business opportunities. The alienation of the farms, while felt by earlier generations, now became a compelling frustration. The city sophistication shown by the new urban resident became the envy of country cousins, and as urban communities increased in number and importance, many farmers had a sense of isolation. The concentration of population was attended by a significant concentration of wealth. In 1890 the average wealth of the rural resident was $3,250, while the average wealth of the city resident was $9,000.[6]

Although the spectacular growth rates for urban areas occurred at the turn of the century, the greatest migration in actual numbers occurred after World War II. The 1940 to 1970 postwar movement to cities totaled 27 million people, a population movement greater than that which brought 21 million Europeans to America between 1890 and 1920. An important component of this postwar migration was the mass movement of blacks from the villages of the South to northern cities. A common thread to all mass migrations in U.S. history has been a search for economic opportunity. This was true for the nineteenth-century pioneers as well as the southern blacks in this century. During this century, 50 percent of the entire nonwhite population above 20 years of age has moved from the South to metropolitan areas in the North and West.[7] The black population of Los Angeles, for example, grew from 75,000 in 1940 to 650,000 in 1965.[8]

This desouthernization and urbanization of the blacks is most remarkable. In 1940 slightly more than one-third of all blacks lived on farms in fifteen southern states. By 1960 that proportion had declined to 7.5 percent.[9] The direct complement of the decline of the southern black farm population was the urban growth outside the South. The nonsouthern urban black population doubled between 1940 and 1960, rising from 11 million to 22 million.[10]

The characteristics and motivations of rural to urban migrants during the first half of this century indicate an economic or career orientation. The migrant tended to be above average in education and occupational skills at his point of origin. In fact, many surveys show that he ranked higher educationally than the population already in the cities.[11] That is, migrants tend to possess higher levels of educational attainment than do nonmigrants. When data are broken down into groups by age, sex, or race, studies indicate that migrants among national regions exhibited higher levels of educational attainment than did nonmigrants residing either at place of origin or destination.

The age grouping of urban migrants was heavily concentrated in the late teens and early twenties. The youthful and vigorous nature of the migrant created a dynamic spirit in the urban region. Immediate sacrifices in living and working conditions were tolerated in consideration for job opportunities with high wages. Migrants of the early 1900s were also attracted by the image of the city as a place of action. An extensive study by Kiser of St. Helena Island, South Carolina, in 1928 showed that religious, racial, and political consideration played little part in migration. The Kiser report found that most men and women from St. Helena were imbued with the idea that to move to the city was to find "good jobs and a more stimulating environment."[12]

The magnetism or opportunity of the new environment was the overriding factor in motivating a move. The mere fact that a person lived in a low-income city or was dissatisfied with his present environment was a secondary factor in the decision to move. Individuals became aware of different levels of living which appeared more attractive and became restless with the level of living in their locale. This considerations, along with a hope that life would be better in a new location, was present in most decisions to move.

The pull-area theory, wherein people tend to be pulled to available jobs rather than pushed, has been shown to be applicable to the rural to urban movement. Knowledge of regional job demands appears to be greater than would be expected. This pull-area theory is also supported by a comprehensive Columbia University survey on the movement of Puerto Ricans. It was found that 59 percent of Puerto Ricans reported that job opportunities was the principal reason they moved to New York.[13]

The migration to cities is also related to business cycles. The University of Pennsylvania study also showed that over a span of seven decades, net migration to and within the United States responded positively and significantly to decadal swings in the economic activity, increasing in periods of prosperity and falling off in periods of depression.[14]

A review of the rationale for migrations appears to put to rest the argument that if a town improves its living conditions and public services too energetically, it will simply see its resources consumed by a rush of new poor, dependent migrant and problem families. First, living conditions and public services play only a small part in determining the number of migrants who move to any particular city. Second, migrants who tend to favor cities are generally from motivated and vigorous elements in the population.

The great urban movement of the nineteenth century was to cities of concentration and centralization. Steam power had totally altered the internal patterns of the city. Before the steam era, few cities exceeded 100,000 population. The great cities emerged with the industrial revolution and the age of steam. Steam was most cheaply produced in large quantities. Thus steam power encouraged the proximity of factory and power supply and fostered the concentration of manufacturing processes. This in turn tended to concentrate the population near the factories. As late as 1899, the average commuting in New York from home to place of work was roughly two blocks, or a quarter of a mile,[15] and over 50 percent of Chicago's 1,690,000 residents lived within 3.2 miles of the city center.[16]

Introduction of farm machinery, which rendered unprofitable much of the agricultural labor of the Old World, enhanced the nearby city as a place of work for the peasant toiler. Jobs and economic gain were in the city. Limited communication and media made the city a cultural, educational, and entertainment oasis, while the rural areas suffered cultural as well as physical isolation.

Post-World War II Growth

The post-World War II urban movement once again created a great demand for consumer goods. Unused capacity of urban industries began to be operated at full capacity, manufacturing civilian goods after the war. The increased use of automobiles and better highways allowed greater separation between place of work and residence. Many urban residents had the opportunity to live in a decent environment while working at a factory which was located in an industrial area. This life-style resulted in mushrooming suburbs. The 1950s and 1960s saw continued vitality for the metropolitan areas. The deterioration of the central city, however, started to become noticeable during these decades. Abandoned buildings and deteriorating neighborhoods began to show their ugly face in scattered areas throughout the inner city. Little attention was given to these blemished city areas until the urban riot explosions of 1968. The aftermath saw the Kerner Commission, a presidential study, warn of two separate societies based on race. Disintegrating areas of the cities were starting to show a breakdown in the perpetual confidence of the city, morale was shaken, and stagnation of growth appeared to be on the horizon.

In the 1970s, statistics started to make clear that great metropolitan areas had stopped growing. Many large northern metropolitan areas are on the edge of bankruptcy. Heavy infusion of federal aid has mitigated the crisis. However, any student who scrutinizes the balance sheets of the large cities soon realizes their precarious fiscal conditions. The nation collectively and individuals more specifically who are trapped in the city are paying enormous social costs.

The social cost of underemployment and unemployment in the city as industry leaves is immeasurable. In a nation where productivity is declining, loss resulting from mislocated labor pools in the city is significant. This social cost has impact at numerous levels. The educational process located in marginal neighborhoods in financially floundering cities suffers. The training obtained in such an environment often fails to prepare the student for even the lowest-level occupations required in a technological age. With fragile fiscal resources, city schoolteachers are now facing payless pay days. Pathetic pleas are made to state governments for financial assistance. Patchwork finances are attempted; however, the municipal school systems continue to deteriorate. A second social cost is a greater demand for social welfare payments due to an excess of workers. The most practical way to lower this welfare load is to reduce the number of excess workers located in the city.

The trapped resident located in a fished-out metropolitan area requires the most important possession of the postindustrial age: knowledge. While collection of knowledge data has become a sophisticated function of most organizations, the underemployed city resident does not know where to get job information. His usual source is unreliable, fragmentary information from friends and neighbors. A pool of information on the current movement of population widely disseminated would provide relief from the culture of poverty. We should consider the use of computerized job banks. This procedure would provide current information on job openings so that the potential relocatees can be presented with a definite job with an identifiable employer, rather than just a possible place or possible employer.

It is necessary to recognize that the reality of a deteriorating area does not preclude job opportunities elsewhere. The implementation by the Department of Labor of numerous job-information outlets in areas of lagging employment is necessary. While professional and technical occupations have sophisticated employment firms with long lists of available jobs in various areas of the country, the industrial worker has no such organization. Job-availability counseling is more rational and cost efficient than make-work projects in high-employment areas. As part of this program, travel subsidies to available jobs could be offered. These travel subsidies would be only a fraction of the cost of money spent on make-work employment, such as the federal CETA program. This travel grant may provide the incentive to carry an unemployed or underemployed person over the threshold and to move him to a more productive life.

It is time to recognize that the magic of centrality has waned and that our fixation with the old concept of the city where jobs are abundant and wages are high no longer provides an accurate view. A more efficient distribution of workers based on accurate job-availability knowledge will lessen the social cost and make both the smaller town and the larger metropolis better places to live and work.

10 The City Today

Life in the city has become a symbol of the fact that man can become adapted to starless skies, treeless avenues, shapeless buildings, tasteless bread, and joyless celebration.—René Dubos

The metropolitan region is ill. It suffers from a multiplicity of problems, some of which may be incurable. It is obvious even to the casual observer that the old structural city is decaying. Often these urban problems are considered to be limited to the central city. Although certain social problems and functional dilemmas are popularly conceived as belonging solely to central cities, in fact no problem can be understood in an isolated analysis of downtown. Traffic jams, for example, do not result from the peculiar design of downtown roads, but from regional systems of work, residents, and transportation. Racial segregation and the loss of business in central cities are not due to some disease found there, but to an urban system and technological factors which encourage escape for those who can afford it.

The consideration of slum districts alone is not an adequate portrait of urbanism, nor is it helpful for understanding the slums. Understood regionally, slums are not a matter of blight but a matter of distribution of wealth and opportunity. This essential interdependence is recognized by perceptive scholars who have analyzed the problems of the city. The metropolitan area as a whole and more specifically the central cities take on similarities to the rural areas during their out-migration era. In the 1960s, for example, four-fifths of the counties in West Virginia declined in population, with seven out of ten young people departing before their twenty-fourth birthday.[1] The impact of non-growth now impacting metropolitan areas is similar to the decline endured by the nonmetropolitan areas for the previous fifty years. Selective out-migration and economic stagnation are self-reinforcing processes and difficult to counteract. Symptoms of the disease are found in the precarious financial position of our metropolitan centers, the rigidity of residential living patterns, the lack of citizen participation, and the inhospitable living environment, caused in large part by the invasion of the automobile.

Studies have shown that out-migration has had profound influence on the economic viability of the area of exit. While most studies have dealt with rural out-migration, the same effects will impact stagnating urban areas.

The usual syndrome results in the least educated and economically productive portion of the population choosing to stay. In the case of rural out-migration areas, it was found that the best educated and most adaptable part of population tends to leave. In 1970, for example, 45 percent of the rural population aged 25 or older had eight years or less education compared with 25 percent of the same group in metropolitan areas.[2]

The out-migration areas tend to have fewer persons under age 35 and more residents 55 or older.[3] As a result, unemployment is higher. Some workers stop looking for work, while others are forced to accept whatever low-paying job is available locally. White-collar workers are underrepresented. The area becomes less attractive to new industries looking for a supply of skilled workers, and more attractive to older lower-wage industries in search of unskilled labor. Since the stagnating area does not attract younger and better educated persons, a lack of vibrancy becomes apparent. The self-reinforcing process of economic stagnation and decline is difficult to combat with increasingly limited resources available to areas of out-migration.

The Fiscal Dilemma of Urban Centers

American cities are economic creatures. As their economic purpose wavers, their attraction fades and their population levels start to recede. This phenomenon has occurred in the central cities since 1950. The somber specter of abandonment and unmaintained buildings and houses is pervasive in large cities. Employment losses lead to population losses, which lead in turn to the disappearance of consumer markets. The aggregate income in 1973 of individuals who moved out of central cities between 1970 and 1974 was about $53.3 billion, while for those moving in it was $25.7 billion, a loss of almost $30 billion due to migration.[4] A change of this magnitude confirms the underlying reasons for the rapid physical deterioration. It is obvious that the capacity to support previous levels of commercial activity is diminished by the lower level of disposable income.

This loss of purchasing power and the deterioration of real property tax base makes higher taxation necessary. Higher taxation, however, renders the environment less hospitable to employers and encourages residents to move to other regions. The young and well-to-do are leaving the aged, unemployed, and minorities in the city. The only alternative is reduction in expenditures. This is difficult when police, fire, and social service departments have an increasing demand on their services. A reduction in services further reduces an already eroding quality of life and often creates more problems than it solves. Hostility arises when salary cutbacks are made on middle-income public servants. Clashes between government administration and service employees have already become a regular feature of metropolitan politics. Striking garbage and mass-transit employees further destroy suitable housing environments. Also salary reduction is merely a short-range solution in a society with persistent inflation.

The fiscal crisis in New York may very well become the norm for other declining metropolitan regions. An economic decline becomes a self-fulfilling prophecy. Up to this point, the decline in the central city was muted because of the economic surge on the suburban fringes. The solution appeared to be redistribution of wealth and expansion. However, when the entire area is stagnating or in decline, there is no obvious solution. The inexorable descent which has occurred in central cities will work itself in a large area. However, the fall will probably be slower.

The symptoms of this decline are lack of long-term investment in property. Insurance companies and banks provide mortgages only to properties that will be viable during the term of the loan. A thirty-year loan in a stagnated or abandoned neighborhood is a poor risk from an investment point of view.

Rigidity of Living Patterns

The names of Lake Forest, Cicero, and the South Side of Chicago create a mental image of the resident. The suburban migration laid the groundwork for the separation of population. This locational process is acting as a giant centrifuge which separates population into concentric layers by income, race, and social class. The resulting isolation provides an effective barrier to gradualistic forms of social interaction, social adjustments, and integration. Hostility and increasing emotional distance between city and suburb are already clear. The most obvious result is an increased division and an even more pronounced emphasis on racial character.

To a great degree, the suburbs have halted the cosmopolitan spirit of social interchange with diverse personalities. The traditional view of the move from the static, provincial countryside to an environment of economic and social variety has almost been laid to rest. The concentric layers or the mosaic landscape precisely define areas for race and economic similarities. This segregation is so defined that many moves in a megalopolis are a result of rises in income. The insidious nature of gradient neighborhoods breeds mistrust and fear which are inflamed during periods of crisis. This isolation shatters the myth of urban tolerance because it causes the majority of people to be judged by the outward appearance. The emphasis on materialism, nationalism, and sartorial symbolism is exaggerated. Failure of wide-ranging personal relationships creates undue emphasis on role playing and a faceless society. The slower-paced life where people take time to talk to one another is lost in the press of getting ahead.

The Automobile and the City

The metropolitan region, characterized by sprawl, lack of open space, and lack of patterns, is largely the result of the predominance of the auto. The automobile has shaped our cities and rules over them. Very little forethought was given in America to the impact of the automobile, other than facilitating utmost mobility for the new invention. There was simply no research on how to build and where to build the roads until the 1930s, by which time traffic patterns and traffic jams had already been established as a major problem. An early 1930s study determined the basic motif for urban highway design: a wheel with the downtown area inside and with highways radiating to the rim.[5] Ability to handle heavy traffic, emphasis on maximum safety at high speeds, curves at gentle angles, moderate grades, and lines of long sight without intersections were the bywords for highway construction. Fulfillment of these requirements demanded a huge right-of-way for the highways and made them a destructive force in the inner city.

The first major highway act was the Federal Highway Act of 1956 which created the interstate highways. While these interstate highways did disperse the American city, it appears that no other goal other than maximizing mobility was considered. Highway engineers did not consider creation of a new form of city or the solution of any social problems associated with the predominance of the automobile.

The effect of such utilitarian highway building without any consideration for social impact is illustrated by Constance Green's description of Detroit:

> Perhaps no city better exemplifies the consequences of sacrificing everything to the automobile. One-hundred-year-old elms and maples came down to make space for the many-lane highways intersecting the circles which Augustus Woodward had laid out for the frontier town of 1803. New towering office buildings crowded the stretches near the waterfront or stood cheek by jowl with low-profile automobile plants flanked fore and aft by asphalt parking lots. While much of the central business district exuded the aura of massive power, from there outward, the miles of repair shops, tacky-looking stores, and squat apartment house blocks conveyed a sense of irredeemable drabness. Pleasant houses set in wide lawns that line quiet streets disappeared before 1930.[6]

The widespread use of the automobile intensified the nineteenth-century urbanization trends. The incredible speed with which the auto and the concomitant highway dominated the American transportation scene must be termed revolutionary. The most obvious effect is the spread of the city in the form of low-density suburbs. The sheer numbers of automobiles in the United States have an obvious impact. Between 1900 and 1910, the number of automobiles in the United States was 8,000; in 1920, 9 million; in 1930, 26 million; in 1960, 87 million; and the estimate for 1980, over 100 million.[7] The overall number of cars continues to rise dramatically as does the proportion of population owning them. California, for example, has more car registrations than the entire continent of South America.[8]

The impact of such numbers on the physical and social form of the system has been immense. York Wilbern comments: "It is difficult for us to realize that this new [automobile] revolution may have a social impact comparable to that of the first [urban revolution]. The basic purpose of the city is the facilitation of interchange . . . when the means of interchange are drastically altered, the nature of the city must also be drastically altered."[9]

The physical form of the city has been altered by the automobile's sheer demand for space. A standard-size car with a driver takes up more than nine times as much space per person in motion than a public conveyance. The space demanded by an automobile, of course, includes parking as well as motion. Two-thirds of Los Angeles' downtown is already given over to the automobile, approximately 33 percent to parking lots and garages and the rest to roads and highways.[10] Los Angeles is a prototype of the essentially modern system. But such is the radical impact of the car that the figures are similar for even older American cities. The space taken over by the automobile is lost to the city as taxable property or building sites. Places like Los Angeles depend crucially on the private car. But that dependence is not natural. It is the result of decades of public policy. It hardly needs demonstrating that government policy discriminates in favor of automobiles. Each year the United States spends ten times as much on highway construction as on mass transportation.[11]

The nature of the automobile is at odds with the nature of the traditional city: the city, that is, in its traditional bounded self-contained form. Los Angeles represents the new American metropolis spreading and indefinable rather than bounded and self-contained as the metropolitan area of the past. The automobile is unquestionably a decentralizing force, chafing against the tendency of the city to centralize business and population. As Lewis Mumford stated in *The City in History*: "When traffic takes precedence over all other urban functions it can no longer perform its own role, that of facilitating meeting and intercourse. The assumed right of the private citizen to go anywhere in the city and park anywhere is nothing less than a license to destroy the city."[12]

Citizen Participation

The factor which is immediately obvious when talking to residents of large metropolitan areas is their feeling of remoteness from political power and an expression of insignificance regarding their efforts to get governmental action. This is often put into the terminology of, "You can't fight city hall." This widespread apathetic attitude is spread throughout the general urban population.

What is often tossed off as apathy, lack of interest in community, and failure to vote may be a logical consequence of our large and complex scale of living. It requires a level of sophistication and wide-range information to understand the complex systems of large cities. Such elevated knowledge is not available to the masses. Decisions are made increasingly by bureaucratic experts, a small elite group with access to the required information. These decisions are increasingly made in secrecy, behind an effective shield of public relations. An intelligent and conscientious citizen cannot decipher the technical information needed to make informed judgments. Inadequate access to the decision maker is a problem endemic to large-scale bureaucratic society. It cannot be solved by calling for open government. The issues are so complex in large-scale systems that government is increasingly dominated by experts who are outside the usual checks and balances of the political process, as they are not elected and generally not publicized.

The perceptual attributes of the modern large-scale metropolis also tend to trivialize citizen participation in subtle ways. Cities have traditionally been seats of power, whether of kings or churches; and this power has often been expressed architecturally. It is sometimes thought that the grand cathedrals and palaces were impressive in their symbolic and actual power over the populace. However, this was a grandeur that could be identified with; it symbolized human power or common values. The modern metropolis is too diffuse to represent grandeur; moreover, its architecture tends to be premised on economy, efficiency, and sterility. To the extent it contains grand images, these are generally utilitarian structures: airports, bridges, expressways, skyscrapers, dams, and reservoirs. Blumenfeld noted that these structures are "extra human."[13] They are products not of human hands, but of mechanical forces of nature controlled by humans. They are generally perceived not in walking or standing, but from a rapidly moving mechanical vehicle. Because the perceptual environment has moved beyond the human scale, it diminishes human importance.

The importance of limited numbers in functional democracy was perceived long ago by Aristotle when he dictated the size of the polis. To Rousseau, opportunities for citizens to participate effectively in making decisions always vary inversely with size; the larger the number of citizens, the smaller the average citizen's share in the decision.[14] Equality, participation, effective control over government, political rationality, friendliness, and civic consciousness decline as the population and territory of a state increase. In our present society, where marketing and politics are carried on in a national arena, it is hard to guarantee that local democracy will function optimally on the community-size level. Nevertheless, there is evidence that civic participation and community identification are significantly higher in smaller towns than in large cities. Robert Dahl suggests the size for contemporary American cities is 50,000 to 200,000, "which even taking the larger figure, may be within the threshold for wide civic participation."[15] Needless to say, our major urban systems have already far outgrown this threshold.

The tremendous size of our nation's metropolitan areas has created a huge separation between urban residents and municipal government. This gap in the relation between residents of large cities and their local governments has resulted in frustrated residents and inefficient government. The performance or lack of performance in school systems, zoning laws, and traffic patterns affect residents more concretely and more fundamentally than most decisions made on the state and national levels.

The most obvious manifestation of citizen participation in municipal government is the publicly held city council meeting. It is often the case, however, that citizens feel their participation in these public hearings to be ineffectual. In many instances, it seems as if a decision has already been reached before the public is even consulted. Problems of metropolitan areas, therefore, seem to move out of everyone's control. The consequences and ramifications of any decision often seem too far-reaching and complex to be easily understood and solved. Faced with a tangle of interlocking needs and problems, complex and foreboding government agencies, urban residents are often reduced to feelings of frustration and powerlessness in their attempts to affect the decisions of local governments.

The widening gap between urban residents and urban government also creates problems for the governing bodies themselves. Because of the tremendous size of the urban areas which they must administer, officials cannot intimately know all the districts that they are governing; often they are unaware of the specific problems of a specific district. This lack of knowledge, coupled with limited citizen access to city administrators, results in governmental inefficiency. Decisions based on incomplete knowledge and partial understanding often fail to solve problems, and they sometimes actually serve to create new, unforeseen problems.

This lack of coordination and inefficiency has bloated the bureaucracy. While ostensibly the enlarged departments are able to handle problems more intimately, the fact is that most decisions are directed from the top. Large departments of administrators inevitably result in standard procedures which turn into what is disparagingly called red tape. The very departments designed to provide access for the citizens become a barrier.

There is also a tendency for the department heads to spend the major part of their time administering their departments. Time spent in policymaking and personnel selection is a further cause of remoteness from the citizen. The ever-expansive government has been and can only be restrained by a smaller government institution.

City government officials are attempting to deal with the problems of a metropolis, despite the fact that available governmental institutions have become anachronistic. One such historical change affecting municipal governments is the tremendous increase in the responsibilities which cities have been forced to accept. Local governments have moved into totally new fields of service. These new activities have created problems not only with respect to the administration of the new programs, but also in coordinating new and old services. Second, expansion in population has necessitated a corollary expansion in municipal bureaucracies. Taken together, these changes have resulted in a vertical division of municipal government along functional lines, which in turn has created governmental incoherence and chaos. Each division may know its own problems, but no one is in a position to conceptualize and coordinate the city as an organic whole.

The most important aspect of civic education in democracy is based on the learning experience. When that experience is frustrating, unproductive, and peripheral to decisions, as is often the case in our American cities, the citizen learns that participation is not a judicious expenditure of time, or that his views do not matter. Consequently, tendencies toward civic apathy and political alienation are enhanced by the existing processes of large-scale governments.

The American City and Blacks

The great bulk of recent migrants to the city were American blacks. From 1900 to 1950, the percentage of blacks outside the South increased from 10 to 30 percent; the percentage within the city rose from 17 to 48 percent.[16] This spreading migration, along with racial prejudice, housing policy, and highway construction, has been an ever-increasing segregation of blacks within the American urban society. Racial segregation intensified due to the fact that twentieth-century American cities were increasing their economic and cultural segregation. Wealthier and more powerful members of the communities moved to the outer zones of the city into new suburban areas. Black colonies were created within the inner city. These environments were not dictated by choice; they were environments dictated by racial discrimination and economic necessities, and they severely limited the chance of upper mobility.

The majority of the central-city residents became separated from the resources of the metropolitan areas. Locating in central areas which are paradoxically the most distant from wealth, educational opportunity, and employment, blacks have become increasingly isolated. Local governments seldom have jurisdiction over the entire metropolitan areas. Fragmentation of the governmental power results in the lack of resources in those localities having the most dire need. Wealthier suburban localities continue to fight proposals for metropolitanwide government. Even proposals to tax suburban commuters to the central city, thus initiating the minimal redistribution of resources, has been soundly defeated in a metropolitanwide election. Isolated emotionally as well as economically, the poor increasingly occupy the central-city "islands," cut off from the freedom of opportunity of mainstream America.

Conclusion

Although as a technological achievement, it may, at one point, have represented a triumph, today's city must be considered an ecological regression. One might ask of a modern city that it be humane, that it be capable of supporting minimal life-style. Cities should be able not only to support the physiological person, but also to give meaning and expression to the person as an individual, as a member of a democratic society. The modern city inhibits the person as a social being and as a spiritual being. It does not offer minimum conditions for the physiological person.

Our heritage of agrarianism, privatism, and suburbanization, and the impact of the automobile have created an intensively urbanized system, a system that appears to lack meaningful definition of either city or country. Growth of our cities was sparked almost entirely by economic factors, and the dominance of these factors has created an expanding metropolis without a real community or solidarity. One author noticed the paradox of living in a system, "marked by rampant urbanization but lacking real cities."[17] To the extent that our metropolitan areas lack vitality and civic consciousness, they must be seen as a reflection of American values. There is overwhelming evidence that Americans today do not identify with metropolitan living. It is obvious that there is a substantial deterioration of the central cities, and the statistics of the 1970s indicate that entire metropolitan region are starting to decline. The decaying areas are characterized by poor-quality housing, low-income residents, and housing abandonment. Causes of deterioration are numerous. The sheer decline of physical structures owing to old age, white flight from integration, and increase in personal incomes which allow some to fortunately find new housing in outlying regions, cause a decline in the older neighborhoods. Only the rich and powerful escape urban tension because their well-protected institutions and cosmopolitan style enable them to pretend that they are not part of the same world as the bulk of the city residents.

There have been numerous prescriptions by urban physicians. Prescriptions of rehabilitation and eradication of substandard buildings given the illusion of healing. It is time to stop tinkering with the existing mechanism in hopes that these minor interventions will turn the city around. Instead, urbanologists should be analyzing deep-seated market forces and long-term social processes. They must begin to understand the dynamic virility of the American economy and its citizens who have little patience in areas which do not provide opportunity.

It cannot be, as Kahn and Wehner predict, that: "The United States of the year 2000 will see at least three gargantuan metropolises, Boswash, Chipitts, and Sansan, which should contain more than half of the United States' population, including an overwhelming proportion of the most prosperous and creative element of society."[18]

The American spirit will not tolerate a deteriorating economic and environmental climate. People leave areas where they are living because they perceive better opportunities for themselves and their families elsewhere. This has been shown in the migration of farmers to the cities, the European immigration to the American shore, and the exodus of poor Southerners to the North. The same impetus which caused early mass migrations is at the heart of the move from the cities.

11 The Metropolis of the Future

What is a city but the people. —Shakespeare

The future of the city will depend on a recognition of its distinctive functions and the development of its positive features. The city has a great deal to contribute toward a satisfying and stimulating environment. A changing perception of quality of life offers the possibility of structuring future metropolitan areas around human needs, rather than simply the needs of industry, as was the case in the past.

The endorsement of dispersal does not quid pro quo mean the decline or deterioration of metropolitan areas. In fact, the phenomenon of dispersal will present unique opportunities for metropolitan areas to rejuvenate and restructure.

The core area of the city possesses museums, zoos, symphonies, the legitimate theater, and major sports attractions. It is the Mecca for cultural activities and first-class entertainment. It is also the center for the communications industry and such support services as advertising and public relations firms. Metropolitan areas have also traditionally served as financial centers. As long as we are a society of private investment, the importance of financial institutions will remain. The decision of who will get the slice of the investment pie will continue to draw the borrowers to the lenders. This type of activity, while enticing some financial employees to live in the central city, is also notable because of the constant flow of clientele which it draws to the city. This is an important function and must continue to be nurtured.

There are, however, certain metropolitan possessions which are no longer appropriate. For example, the large manufacturing or industrial plant located in close proximity to residential neighborhoods is an archaic combination. The amalgamation of the industrial use to residential areas hastens the decay of an urban neighborhood. As we saw in earlier chapters, the location of industry in nonmetropolitan areas is clearly the trend. While relocation of this industry may cause short-term labor adjustments, in the long run it will prove beneficial to the metropolis.

A revolutionary call for abandonment or total rejection of the city would needlessly polarize. Fierce opposition would arise from many sectors of society. This confrontation would blind both the advocates of dispersal and the anti-dispersalists from recognizing and developing the distinctive functions provided by the city. The city has a role to play which should be acknowledged and pursued. Cities should retain those functions which absolutely require physical conglomerations and surrender those which do not.

This chapter describes the future environment of the cities. It explores the new patterns of metropolitan life and the concept of recycling neighborhoods, and identifies who will be the future urban resident.

New Patterns of Metropolitan Life

To an increasing extent, large industries are moving out of the nation's metropolitan areas. As pointed out earlier, the industrial emigration has resulted from changes in factors of production which make it more profitable for industry to locate in nonmetropolitan areas.

It was once thought that an industrial plant had to be located in the midst of a large labor pool. It has become increasingly clear that the location of industrial plants in small towns will attract the necessary labor from a large surrounding area. General Motors, for example, located 1,500 to 2,500 employee facilities in towns with 5,000 to 15,000 population and found that it can obtain the labor force to support these plants.

The corollary to the reduced presence of industries in large cities is the reduction in the industrial labor pool. The blue-collar worker, often noncosmopolitan in nature, will have less and less of a problem picking up stakes and moving to new growth areas. While we have seen that economic opportunity is not as powerful a motivation as it once was, urban blue-collar workers are still strongly economically motivated. Once information of job opportunities in other areas becomes common knowledge, increased out-migration will occur in this group which will have a significant impact on the social makeup of the city.

The new urban environment will be characterized by a certain smallness. Functional differentiation, interdependence, and diversity which have been associated with metropolitan life will continue to draw. People who have a fundamental affection for diversity will continue to seek the urban environment. A large city has certain qualities which are supportive of smaller-scale and specialty enterprises. First, a certain economy of scale is prerequisite for smaller-scale and specialty businesses. Second, skills and services available in the city are supportive since the small-scale business is not self-sufficient. The small-scale business requires others to supply it with skills and services. This interdependence allows a greater specialization since a jack-of-all-trades is no longer necessary. The future growth of the service industries will be strongly affected by the diversity of the city. Increased specialization causes increased interdependence, which in turn creates the requirement of additional services.

The new residential environment will be characterized by a more human scale. Residential areas will have more parks and green space instead of block after block of solid housing. The city will become more civilized. Its artificial environment and density will thin. While density will continue in the center, the area surrounding the core area will allow lower-residential density. This simpler, less artificial environment will be due to the realization that high-rise urbanized living is simply not the most efficient. The efficient and less costly will be the goal.

Future city plans will have lower profiles. The Renaissance Center in Detroit, the Water Tower Place in Chicago, and New York's 100-story Twin Towers are incongruous in the cities when the future demands frugality and simplification. One benefit of these overwhelming structures is the infusion of new pride they bring to the core area. They are symbols of regeneration. Citizens are impressed, believing that technology can triumph. The fact of the matter is that these superstructures have little overall impact on the metropolitan area and are remnants of the surplus technology mentality. Efficiency and simplicity are the bywords of the future.

The metropolis will become more amorphous. The central areas will share with the periphery as distribution of goods and administration is scattered throughout the city. Subcenters which gradually assemble a complex of supportive businesses have sprouted in many larger metropolitan areas. New York, Detroit, and Chicago have all witnessed highly developed business centers outside the central area. Intersections of major freeways or jetports are often the locations for subcenters. These subcenters, which have excellent transportation facilities, compete with the central area. Subcenters often have the advantages of suburban amenities with urban services. As these centers grow and become self-sustaining, the central business district tends to decline in importance. The outlying areas become increasingly independent. Central areas no longer function as a unique location for many of the region's services.

One frightening pattern which seems unavoidable is the fact that the uneducated and poor will find the city a bleak place to live. The jobs of the future are basically professional and technical. Contrary to all logic, huge numbers of unskilled, semiskilled, and blue-collar workers have been concentrated in the metropolitan areas. This is exactly where living and housing costs are often highest, and prospects for meaningful employment are dim. The shrinkage will encourage flight; forced accommodation to new conditions will also cause stress and conflict.

The city is attracting a new, educated middle class in marked contrast to the blue-collar working-class immigrants of the past. This new class will be characterized by working women, smaller families, and close-in residences since the cost in both time and money will make commuting less attractive. This new middle class is increasingly childless, increasingly single, and increasingly desirous of apartment living. As the prosperous middle class seeks housing within the urban area, there will be a displacement of the poor and working class. For the element that is poor, uneducated, and unfit even for clerical jobs, there is little expectation for improvement. The changing job demands of the city are creating the opposite of a labor pool. There could be a generation of unemployables for whom there will be simply no jobs in the city. This group will diminish as they slowly perceive that job demand is elsewhere. The city is simply in no position to be the benefactor of the poor when the market forces contradict. In light of the cities' tenuous financial underpinnings, concentration of the poor in urban areas is untenable and will not persist.

The city will not change overnight. Today's life-style is deeply ingrained. The change will result from external pressure. As energy and resource shortages occur and real estate prices rise, there will be more and more emphasis on preservation and improvement. Preservation and improvement of the existing housing stock will improve the morale, increase the tax base, and start the free-market financial investments to return to the urban neighborhood.

Recycling of Neighborhoods

When parts of the city stop growing, stagnate, and decline, the city looks to the federal government to provide mortgage and rental assistance. The situation is analogous to a junkie frantically jumping at any hope of obtaining drugs. Following this instinctive reflex, cities embark on housing developments taking advantage of federal subsidies in the vain hope that a new building will spark a rebirth.

The infusion of new housing in the slum area is the wrong approach. The slum reflects the misery of its inhabitants, and the improvement of physical surroundings is temporary. New and better housing soon declines to the same tenement condition as its downtrodden neighbors. This fact is a housing corollary to Gresham's law, which can be phrased "that bad housing drives out good housing." To seriously contemplate industry returning to a dying neighborhood or providing a patchwork quilt of public assistance to a deteriorating area is futile.

The inescapable fact is that certain areas of the metropolis are not only ill, but dying or dead. This fact, once confronted, provides a firm base for decision making. These areas allow the possibility of low-density residential or green-space development. To date, there has been a hesitancy or an intentional failure to consider the possibility that terminal neighborhoods should be allowed to die. The urban professional and politician find it painful to admit that a neighborhood is dead. This attrition is actually occurring and demands an explicit policy. Mayors and councilmen, however, studiously ignore the event.

New growth and development of any neighborhood is the established prescription for dying neighborhoods. It is time to face the fact that both the residents of a terminal neighborhood and the urban area as a whole may benefit if the neighborhood is allowed to die.

The fact of the matter is that birth and death of cities and various parts of cities is an integral component of the natural order. Prior to the Department of Housing and Urban Development (HUD) and professional planners, entire towns atrophied and died when their purpose was removed. The residents left and found opportunities in other viable areas.

The better solution is to improve a salvageable neighborhood. Such a neighborhood still has a social integrity along with structurally sound homes. As our country relates to scarcer resources, it will be forced to emphasize remodeling and restoration. A modern mechanical system, better roof, and exterior restoration will become more popular. A nation that has gone so far as to make housing another disposable will be forced to change. No longer will it be economically feasible to commence new construction when existing housing is standing empty merely because of lack of repairs. Rehabilitation and repair of old buildings will provide livable quarters within the existing boundaries. Characteristics of the residents change as neighborhoods upgrade themselves. Recycling is a method that should apply to buildings as well as to cans and bottles.

The parts of the city that can survive should receive preservation subsidies. The subsidies must be directed to areas where conventional financing has a chance to return. These sections still have community support and residents who are dedicated to improvement. Application of funds should be selectively expended in areas with preservation possibilities. The above cirterion for urban diagnosis is subjective. However, urban curative measures have been judgmental and will continue to be even if neighborhood recycling becomes a viable alternative.

The absolute irrationality of placing federally subsidized housing for the poor in urban areas deserves further consideration. In 1979, HUD had allowed up to $60,000 in cost for the new urban dwelling unit and has allowed rental levels in subsidized housing to increase to $1,100 per month. Under the existing section 8 HUD program, the federal government pays the differential between one-quarter of the tenant's income and the fair market rental of up to $1,100. It is thus possible for the government to contribute $1,100 per month to the rental of a $60,000 apartment unit to be occupied by a low-income family.[1]

This has to be compared with the construction of apartments in small towns in the Midwest or South which cost $20,000 per dwelling unit and rent for $250 per month. The differential between $20,000 and $60,000 per unit must be scrutinized and debated by a Congress troubled by chronic inflation. There appears no rational explanation for the same consumer good costing the federal government three times as much merely because of its location in a large city. The expenditure becomes even more suspect when one considers the more expensive dwelling unit is located in depressed areas with minimal redeeming virtues.

The staggering cost of urban living has become a singularly important consideration. No longer can the higher costs of living be justified by the retort that urban incomes are far greater than nonmetropolitan incomes.

National unions have made income relatively uniform, forcing the urban resident to closely examine his expenditures.

In 1979 it was not unusual for a middle-income family to pay $500 or $600 for a moderate apartment unit in New York City. As the cost of living and utility expenses continue to increase in the city along with the disappearance of jobs, relocation to other areas becomes more and more feasible.

A major issue will be whether the poor will be able to find adequate housing in the cities. If it is not available at reasonable prices, there will be little choice but to look outside the metropolitan area. The question of how much in the way of job loss, disamenities, and deterioration of environment before the scales tip in favor of a move is unanswered. There appears to be very little the city or its residents can do to avoid the misery and dislocation in a declining neighborhood. The short-term effects cannot avoid unpleasantness. People who continue to remain in declining or dead neighborhoods are heavily dependent on services and usually undercontribute on taxes.

Neighborhood improvement and pervasive maintenance appear only when the middle-income class of residents move into an area. This phenomenon has been termed *gentrification*.[2] In Chicago, for example, gentrification has occurred in the form of a condominium conversion boom. This phenomenon has resulted in the rehabilitation of many older deteriorating apartment buildings. Rehabilitation markedly upgrades the neighborhood and improves the market value in the immediate vicinity. The rehabilitated dwelling units generally are sold to middle-class residents. Gentrification has occurred at a time when skyrocketing new house prices make older homes and structures in viable neighborhoods more attractive. The architecture, the high-ceiled rooms, the woodwork, and the ornate masonry are irreplaceable and unique, rendering them desirable. Although gentrification and condominium conversion improve older city neighborhoods, the phenomenon is not without criticism. Critics of condominium conversions correctly state that the low-income renter is displaced. However, overall it must be admitted that gentrification is a positive influence in neighborhood improvement and possibly the only real hope for urban renewal.

Up until recent times, the expanding metropolitan region continued to build homes on the periphery. This continued expansion has drawn population from the older homes in the central areas, leaving them to poor families. This is sometimes called the filtering-down process.[3] As expansion of the periphery comes to a halt, central-city houses in certain areas are being restored, thus the older homes traditionally filtering down to the poor are simply not there. The failure to find decently priced housing is another pressure forcing the poor urban resident to consider relocation.

The improvement of the city will not be the result of state and federal statutes barring *red lining*, the term used to describe those sections of the metropolitan area which have been categorized as unloanable by banks. Banks write off a neighborhood because of falling real estate prices, poor credit risks among potential buyers, and skepticism about mortgage payments. In recent years, federal and state governments enacted legislation barring banks from redlining areas. The fact of the matter is that banks are behaving reasonably enough from their own point of view when they make such decisions. If there is little hope of obtaining repayment of capital, they decide to invest in other areas. When banks and major insurance companies voluntarily reverse their policies against investment in certain neighborhoods, the future of the area will be good. Hope and speculation credit are necessary for an area to blossom. This will not happen everywhere; it will only happen in salvable neighborhoods.

These changes will not be due to a formal plan since little in free enterprise America is achieved by plan. Real structural change occurs as a result of the free market mechanism. A demand for a scarce product creates producers. The wrong path is to have the government provide new buildings in slum areas. Free market experts have already written this off as a poor investment. Pressure groups often criticize the free market as failing to perform. The alleged failure of the free market to perform is in fact the rational decision that the investment dollars or mortgage loans will never be recaptured.

The stark reality is that before an area will be upgraded or maintained, community banks must make the decision that the area has potential. A mere declaration by HUD that a bank must invest in a slum or marginal neighborhood is diametrically opposed to good banking practices. The result of such an edict is usually a feigned or token compliance by the bank. This Sword of Damocles held over a banker's neck will not provide stable neighborhoods. The free market mechanism, where residents invest in homes and condominiums, is the only answer. Their vote for maintaining and improving the neighborhood will prove to be far more fruitful than coercive rules and regulations promulgated by the government forcing banks to lend in deteriorating areas.

The subsidization of lower-income families must occur only in environments which are salvageable. Proponents of selective neighborhood rehabilitation are charged with benign neglect or letting certain neighborhoods die. The recognition that these neighborhoods are dead is preferable to a hollow endorsement of saving every neighborhood.

The adjustment to working with a declining population may have some beneficial side effects for the metropolis. There will be fewer children in school, which may allow far more intensive teaching. A depopulation will find fewer teenagers to contribute to the crime rate. As older people become a larger segment of the population, transportation congestion should be relieved. There would be fewer urban renewal projects uprooting old communities. It may well be that there will be a more stable, reliable community. No-growth does not have to be synonomous with impoverishment.

At the end of his book, Ebenezer Howard asks what will happen to London as a result of this depopulation. He pictures falling land values, falling rents, and decrease in density. London gradually becomes attractive. It appears a certain amount of unloading of population will be necessary before the city can offer enough amenities to become attractive.

The Metropolitan Resident of the Future

The only solution of permanence is an urbane citizenry who prefer to be located in a metropolitan area. As the city is becoming increasingly dominated by professional, technical, and clerical occupations, it is attracting different people than during the earlier industrial era. The recent urban migrant has a penchant for metropolitan life and is not drawn simply to a job. There are certain common characteristics in the new residents which bode well for the future of the city. This chapter attempts to identify certain types of residents who will be a positive influence, eventually transforming and stabilizing the city into a livable environment.

One important segment of recent immigrants to the city are the upwardly mobile, childless, sophisticated, tolerant, and interdependent citizens. The ambience of the city gives the young professional or technician the sense of liberation and largess that he is seeking. There appears to be a definite age bias toward individuals in their twenties and thirties. This group has definite preference for working and living in the central city. Such individuals readily accept dense neighborhoods. However, they also demand that their neighborhoods be pleasant. This group is pragmatic, well read, and fervent in support of the cosmopolitan life-style.

Another group with strong bias toward metropolitan living is composed of individuals who have a life-style drastically different from the norm. This genre includes artists and radicals. Eccentricity is allowed and even encouraged in the residential area where these specialized life-styles congregate. The large city is amenable to their life-style. It allows them a relativistic perspective since the urban environment is sprinkled with divergent personalities and life-styles.

Still another group is the young families who enjoy the cosmopolitan air of the city and are dedicated to the rehabilitation of a house. This group must be distinguished from the upwardly mobile, organizational person. A representative of this group is often a craftsperson involved in a small specialized business who tends to be intellectual and introspective. His scorn of large corporations and suburban life propels him to the inner-city area of the metropolitan region. The rehabilitation of an inner-city house, often a significant avocation, becomes a preoccupation. Such young cosmopolitans are ready personally to work to create a favorable atmosphere. Their presence attracts other vibrant citizens.

The leisure class is yet another group which has a high preference for the city. This constituency consists of families with established wealth and leaders in the corporate hierarchy. This group can afford the best, and the plethora of services, entertainment, and culture located in the city's central area attracts them.

Recent immigrants to America form yet another large important group within the cities. Immigrants, both past and present, tend to concentrate in large cities, where ethnic grouping occurs and the need for low-skilled workers exists. When the metropolitan area was expanding, the foreign immigrants were easily assimilated economically, socially, and culturally into the urban society. This no longer holds true.

The preservation of the ethnic areas in large cities is rapidly coming to a close. The comfort of locating in a large Polish or German neighborhood after leaving the homeland was a magnet for the big cities. As ethnic neighborhoods in a large city no longer provide a powerful attraction, immigrants may consider the availability of jobs instead of automatically moving to the metropolis. Immigration authorities in recent years have instituted regulations which often require a job placement prior to allowing immigration.

Although it appears that the flow of foreign migrants to the metropolitan area will continue, it will be a smaller flow. If the job demand is greater in the nonmetropolitan areas, flow to the city will dissipate or the foreign migrant may stay in the city for only a short time. When he finds that available jobs are located in nonmetropolitan areas, he will move.

Conclusion

The metropolitan area's future growth must be built on its foundation of unmatched variety of professional services, location of national financial institutions, communication centers, cultural centers, and international trade centers. Private businesses that have viewed the city as a tool should become active in civic support. The metropolitan area has special advantages in providing selective services to the rest of the country.

Historically, all societies and cultures have had master cities. This is true not only for Western societies. The city is not a recent phenomenon, neither are its malaise and political demise. Toledo in medieval Spain and Vienna as late as the early-twentieth century indicate that cities like civilizations live and decline, if not entirely expire.[4]

The city will face unprecedented short-term problems. The army of unemployables and the death of certain neighborhoods will be more poignant. The metropolis must confront the fact that certain areas will slowly and selectively decline in population. This decline will bring about out-migration causing the city to stabilize at a smaller population. The smaller population, however, will have a core of ardent supporters of city life. Their support will transform the city so that it will provide pleasant living along with its unique possessions. This will in turn attract residents with renewed vigor.

The city's white-collar work force appears to be stable. The downturn in the economy does not throw them out of work. These two activities—those of the white-collar and service or tertiary sector—have now become the characteristic metropolitan activities.

The major changes will occur as traditional housing is upgraded. People have an innate desire for low-density housing with proximity to parks and open spaces. As the population falls and the new areas are determined to be of investment grade, the potential of the city will be realized. The only cure is residents who are located in the urban areas by choice and who are dedicated to the proposition of a livable city.

Along with satisfied citizens, businesses must give active support to urban improvements. The case of the Ford Motor Company is an excellent example of a corporation that invested private dollars in residential and commercial development within the metropolitan area. Ford's residential developments have been in areas which are salvageable and have a future. These investment dollars made on the basis of a hard-nosed business decision in the long run accrue more benefits than a residential investment which is viewed simply as a contribution. Such business investments were based on reasonable investment criteria, not under a threat of federal coercion. Only when businesses and citizens invest because they feel they will recoup in the future will there be a true renaissance in the city.

In the postindustrial era, cities may be left to those who truly love them. It must be determined, therefore, which characteristics of the urban environment are to be retained. This environment will most probably be characterized by a certain smallness. Functional differentiation and the interdependence and diversity which have resulted will be maintained by intellectuals, experimenters, and craftspersons. These people tend to have a fundamental affection for the diversity and stimulation provided by the urban environment. The city will continue to attract talented individuals because it will continue to serve as a catalyst for their interaction. It is in this sense that a vital diversity of urban environment will be preserved.

Urban advocates must search for the means by which the metropolitan areas can continue to serve their unique functions. Solutions to urban problems must be found which preserve the immense, functional variety traditionally present in large cities. It will require encouraged experimentation and creative endeavors to preserve the positive and unique attributes of the metropolitan areas.

12 The Growth Towns of the Future

There is a need for intimate human relationships, for the security of settled home and associations, for spiritual unity, and for orderly transmission of the basic cultural inheritance. These the small community at its best can supply. Whoever keeps the small community alive and at its best during this dark period, whoever clarifies, refines, and strengthens the vision of the small community, may have more to do with the final emergence of a great society than those who dominate big industry and big government.—from the preface to the St. Johnsbury, Vermont, Town Plan

The future of the country lies with an undiscovered natural resource. This discovery will turn no wheels, will produce no more electricity, it is not buried, and will not be discovered by Exxon or Shell. The natural resources of the future are the 312 communities with populations of 50,000 to 500,000 and the 5,000 towns with populations from 2,500 to 5,000.[1]

Most of these smaller cities are strategically located and have the fundamental characteristics to make them nuclei for the development of the kind of environment which can satisfy the broadest scope of human needs. They are located on major highways, rivers, and ports. They have sewer, water, and physical improvements in place. As these small cities grew, they tested various growth lines and matured in accordance with the time-tested values and desires of the city.

The distinct advantage of growth centers over the new town concept is the possession of roots. A stable identification with a city is only developed over a period of years. The fact that social institutions are established provides the security, self-assurance, and concept of perpetuity usually lacking in new towns. The existing centers have been built on the fundamental needs of inhabitants, and the values of their citizens are a known commodity. Clubs, churches, and banks present a matrix of civic pride. Such cities welcome new industry, additional capital improvements, and a larger consumer market. These medium-size cities are the most efficient because various governmental services can be supplied at a lower-cost per capita than in larger metropolitan areas.[2]

The residents in the 5,000 small communities scattered throughout the country have a more intimate association and participation in cultural and political life. The local politicians are neighbors and are recognized in the street. Major civic improvements, since they affect all the citizens more directly, are the norm for morning-coffee conversations. There is no reason why people have to make a daily effort to escape the drabness and the ugliness in the community or neighborhood in which they live, or spend many hours each day driving in an automobile. The relentless growth of a metropolitan region creates the inhuman community form known as sprawl. Statistics clearly show that the larger a metropolitan area is, the longer the average journey to work and the more traffic congestion there will be.[3]

Smaller communities can provide all the fundamental amenities of daily modern life and permit residents to pursue life based on the pursuit of quality and the satisfactions of personal recognition. As the desire for the quality of life grows among metropolitan residents, they will be drawn to the small town growth centers.

The satisfaction with quality of life appears to be highest in small- and medium-size towns. A 1976 study by Luther Tweeten and Yau-Chi Lu concluded that smaller cities hold singular possibilities for satisfaction and feeling of personal effectiveness. It was assumed that a residence was a better or more optimal place to live if people have confidence in the politcal process, are progressive on racial issues, and feel confidence in their personal effectiveness and control of their own lives.[4]

It was found that feelings of personal effectiveness were significantly greater in smaller towns. Not only were attitudes toward segregation favorable in smaller towns, income and education differences of small towns have minimal influence on progressive racial attitudes.

Tweeten and Lu concluded that opportunities for racial integration are enhanced in a smaller city. In nonmetropolitan areas there is often only one high school in the town. The opportunities for integration are obviously greater. There is simply not enough population for an all-black school and an all-white school. The smaller size was also found to cause less isolation between the races. Smaller cities result in neighborhoods, churches, trade areas, and other places closer together, allowing for day-to-day interchange among all citizens. The smaller size simply does not allow the gradation and concentration of economic and social classes in separate neighborhoods to the degree which is found in the metropolitan area. While social and racial mixture has limitations in any size towns, the task of integrating a metropolitan ghetto of 1 million blacks is nearly impossible because it is large enough to constitute a system and culture in itself, as well as being physically isolated from the rest of the city.

As was shown, the isolation of ethnic groups and the necessity to label causes a person in a metropolitan area to be known merely as an Italian or a Pole, rather than as an individual with a unique personality. While racial and social segregation exists in medium-size towns, it is not as pervasive and as all-encompassing. The schools are usually integrated; and the minorities have opportunities to experience at close range the culture, life-style, and attitudes of the majorities and vice versa. This can be distinguished from the metro-politan areas where the minority group often appears to be operating under one principle and culture, while the majority is operating under another.

The rapid decline in the importance of geographic distance and geographic place is significant. This remarkable change from traditional demography raises the medium-size growth center town from its former backwater status. Tradi-tionally, city folks visiting small towns were treated as strangers; styles of living and thinking were much different. Residents of smaller towns gave little notice to national events since they felt their world was distinct and separate.

This pattern has been reversed. The hayseed farmer went out with vaude-ville. Farmers today watch television documentaries and are petite bourgeoisie, overseeing hundreds of thousands of dollars of highly technical agricultural equipment. On the other hand, the new migrants to the city, who are concen-trated in the highest-density sections of the city, are those who exhibit most of the attributes of traditional rural folk. They are the last viable remnant of a preindustrial society where village styles are intact. Here, turf is the city block, where teenage gangs wage war in its defense. The slum blocks in the central cities are the only remaining pure place, social neighborhoods we have left.

The medium-size growth center provides humanistic conceptions of a city, in contrast to anonymous, amorphous conurbations. The simple ability to travel in all sections of the city and walk outside at night is not possible in the tense urban atmosphere. The conurbation is choking with alienated and atomized aggregations of human beings, consisting of privileged white enclaves, and encircled totalitarian cities composed of starved ghettos. The medium-size town is more people-oriented, whereas the metropolitan individual appears to emphasize things. The medium-size growth center does not have as great a tendency to reduce relationships to cash, which thereby tends to remove moral and esthetic constraints.

James Rouse, planning leader and founder of the new town Columbia, who has worked in metropolitan, suburban, and small town environments, eloquently states a case for the growth of smaller towns.

> I believe that many of the most serious problems of our society flow from the fact that the city is out of scale with people; that it is too big for people to comprehend, to feel a part of, to feel responsible for, to feel important in. I believe this out-of-scaleness promotes loneliness, irresponsibility, superficial values. People grow best in small communities where the institutions, which are the dominant forces in their lives, are within the scale of their comprehension and within reach of their sense of responsibility and capacity to manage. A broader range of friendships and relationships occurs in a village or small town than in a city; there is a greater sense of responsibility

for one's neighbor and a greater sense of support by one's fellow man. I believe that self-reliance is promoted, that relationship to nature— to the out-of-doors—to the freer forms of recreation and human activity is encouraged in a smaller community.[6]

It is important to point out that the medium-size town, as a growth center, is a form of dispersal. This is distinct and different from decentralization. Decentralization is linked with the decongestion of the city; however, there is a continual focus on the center. Dispersal is a more comprehensive concept which creates new residential clusters, rather than merely reaching out of the existing urban districts. In the rejuvenation of growth centers, it is important to keep this distinction in mind. Dispersal within the ambit of a metropolitan area does not reduce but often increases the pressure of centralization. Suburbs have become satellite cities guilty of leapfrogging the urban expansion. This again is decentralization rather than dispersal. When separation is thin, the greenbelt becomes susceptible from two directions: the city growing outward and the new town growing inward. Park Forest, Illinois, is an example of a new town espousing concepts of dispersal, while, in reality, it is another decentralized suburban community. By locating on the fringe of Chicago without greenbelts, Park Forest has become interwoven with other southern Chicago suburbs which never held themselves out as new towns.

The critics of dispersal contend that medium-size growth centers will not attract because of the provincial mannerisms and lack of diversity within smaller towns. This criticism has been largely blunted by cultural and social decentralization. The fact that most information is received from the same sources neutralizes the differential. The mannerisms of Americans have become much more dependent on social and economic classification than on geographic location. While there appears to be no escape from a certain amount of centralized information, the medium-size growth center provides the best hope for more humanistic person to person interchange.

Our goal is a balance between the smaller towns and the large cities and suburbs. We have not advocated the eradication of the city. No one city size will satisfy the needs of all the people. The question is one of accommodating to the existing metropolitan structure or changing it. Our hope is for a transformation. The city recomposed with the absence of people who neither desire to be there nor contribute to the city will actually increase the diversity of the city. As the quality of life increases in the city, a new, more diverse, and more vibrant citizenry will be drawn.

Small towns are necessary for the survival of America. The medium-size cities of 5,000 to 500,000 combine the basic amenities along with the preferred life-style. With the days of the pleasure garden rapidly coming to an end, internalization of consciousness will develop. This tendency bodes well for the smaller town in America.

Conclusion

Dispersal of the population will find people locating in towns where a requisite quality of life exists. Population dispersal does not entail a new style of agricultural life. With 4 percent of the population providing adequate agricultural output, the favored locales appear to be the existing small- and medium-size towns. The bulk of the new growth will be in towns with populations ranging from 5,000 to 500,000. Some towns are actually too small; populations less than 2,500 often have problems supplying basic services such as medical care, educational facilities, and utilities.

Medium-size towns offer variety in terms of environment. Smaller towns often have an isolation and insularity where lack of conformity to centralized values is possible. While the metropolitan-based media has penetrated smaller towns, forcing a degree of uniformity, a different life-style in smaller places is still possible. Each small town is special to its residents, and there is a wide range of places where uniqueness can be perceived. Within the smaller towns there are often strong divisions; some residents want to bring in the conveniences of urban society to their community, while others reject the forces that tend to lure them to the urban maelstrom. It is their uniqueness that draws people to them. Vibrant small towns are necessary as an alternative to the city itself. Categorizing them as all alike is unjust. We reject statements such as Jane Jacobs' assertion in *The Death and Life of Great American Cities* that: "Self-sufficient small towns are really nice little towns if you are docile and have no plans of your own."[7]

The issue is not new growth towns versus the city, but revitalized small towns and healthy, restructured large cities. Revitalization of small towns is an integral component of the vanguard we are beginning to know as smaller (appropriate) technology, alternate life-styles, and environmental conservation.

The initial surge of enthusiasm and confidence by smaller cities will shake the morale of metropolitan residents. The metropolitan area stands convicted of second-place attractiveness; often those who stay are dispirited by the migration of friends. America has little experience in shrinking of population, and the affliction now occurring more and more frequently on the metropolitan scene raises a stereotype of deterioration and neglect. The urban resident is not, of course, without alternatives. Much as the displaced and vestigial farmers left the countryside in the first half of the twentieth century, urban residents will be attracted by the new magnetism of the growth centers. It is time to put an end to the frenetic pace where the average American is moving seven times in his lifetime. It is time to get to know one's neighbor, to grow with an identifiable city whose residents are more than numbers.

America is known for its trend-setting and acceptance of the latest fads. Once the growth center becomes where the action is, publicty and favorable acceptance will tap latent energies. Dormant individuals, societies, and associations of medium-size cities will become kinetic. When these medium-size cities gain self-respect and self-confidence, the young will not be lost to the metropolis; the forgotten smaller cities will be rejuvenated.

Notes

Introduction

1. Lewis Mumford, *The Urban Prospect* (New York: Harcourt Brace Jovanovich, 1956) p. 108.

Chapter 1

1. Harry K. Schwarzweller, "Migration and the Changing Rural Scene," *Rural Sociology* 44 (1979):7.

2. Current metropolitan area definition (1975), U.S. Bureau of the Census.

3. U.S. Department of Commerce, Bureau of the Census, "Current Population Reports," Series P-25, no. 640, *Estimates of the Population of States with Components of Change: 1970-1975* (Washington: U.S. Government Printing Office, 1976).

4. Calvin L. Beale, *The Revival of Population Growth in Non-Metropolitan America* (Washington: U.S. Department of Agriculture, Economic Research Service, ERS 605, 1975).

5. Peter Morrison, "Migration and Rights of Access: New Public Concerns of the 1970s," Rand Paper, P-5785, March 1977.

6. David Hacker, "Back to the Boonies: Small Towns Thrive as Urban Migration Reverses," *The National Observer*, 5 January 1974. Reprinted with permission.

7. Peter Morrison, "Population Movements and Shape of Urban Growth: Implications for Public Policy and Population Distribution," in *Report of the Commission on Population Growth in the American Future* (Washington: U.S. Government Printing Office, 1972).

8. Peter Morrison, "Dimensions of the Population Problem in the United States," in *Report of the Commission*, p. 15.

9. "The Mobility of the Population of the United States: March 1970-March 1975" (Washington, D.C.: Bureau of the Census, 1975).

10. Peter Morrison, and Judy P. Wheeler, "Rural Renaissance in America: The Revival of Population Growth in Remote Areas," *Population Bulletin* 31, no. 3, October 1976.

11. "Drift Away from Big Cities," *United States News and World Report*, 15 November 1976.

12. Francis Bonynge, *The Future Wealth of America* (New York, 1852).

13. *Projections of Urban Population, Urban Decline and Rural Increase* (Washington, D.C.: National Resources Committee, October 1937).

14. U.S., the Domestic Council, Congress, Committee on Community Development, "Report on National Growth and Development," 1974.

15. Gallup Opinion Surveys (Princeton: American Institute of Public Opinion, March 1966 and August 1971) report 74.

16. Sarah Mills Mazie and Steve Rawlings, "Public Attitudes toward Population Distribution Issues," in *Report of the Commission*, p. 605.

17. Gallup Opinion Poll (1977), *New York Times*, 2 March 1978.

18. Glen Fuguitt and James J. Zuiches, "Residential Preferences and Population Distribution," *Demography* 12, no. 3 (1975):491-504.

19. Edwin Carpenter, "The Potential for Population Dispersal: A Closer Look at Residential Location Preferences," *Rural Sociology* 42, no. 3 (February 1977):352-370.

20. Gordon DeJong, "Residential Preferences and Migration," *Demography* 14, no. 2 (May 1977):169-178.

21. Niles Hansen, *The Future of Non-Metropolitan America* (Lexington, Mass.: Lexington Books, D.C. Heath, 1973), p. 8.

22. Carpenter "Potential for Population Dispersal," pp. 352-370.

23. John B. Lansing and Eva Mueller, "The Geographic Mobility of Labor" (Ann Arbor: University of Michigan Survey Research Center, 1967).

24. Bureau of the Census, *Statistical Abstract of the United States: 1975* (Washington: U.S. Government Printing Office, 1975), p. 345.

25. Hansen, *Future of Non-Metropolitan America*, p. 8.

26. Bernard L. Weinstein, and Robert E. Firestine, *Regional Growth and Decline in the United States: The Rise of the Sun Belt and the Decline of the Northeast* (New York: Praeger, 1978), pp. 11-19.

27. George Sternlieb and James W. Hughes, "New Regional and Metropolitan Realities of America," *Journal of the American Institute of Planning*, 43 (July 1977):230.

28. Ibid., p. 235.

29. Thomas Muller, "The Declining and Growing Metropolis: A Fisical Comparison," in *Post-Industrial America: Metropolitan Decline and Inter-Regional Job Shifts*, ed. George Sternlieb and James W. Hughes (Center for Urban Policy Research, Rutgers University, 1975), p. 199.

30. Ibid., p. 203.

31. Ibid., p. 216.

32. Ibid., p. 201.

33. Bureau of the Census, "Current Population Reports," pp. 5-24.

34. Muller, "Declining and Growing Metropolis," p. 212.

35. Brian J.L. Berry, "The Decline of the Aging Metropolis: Cultural Bases and Social Process," in *Post-Industrial America*, pp. 175-189.

36. Muller, "Declining and Growing Metropolis," pp. 197-216.

37. Irving Hock, "Urban Scale and Environmental Quality," in *Research Reports of the Commission on Population Growth and the American Future, Population, Resources and Environment* (Washington: U.S. Government Printing Office, 1972), 3:241.

38. Weinstein and Firestine, *Regional Growth*, p. 26.

39. Sternlieb and Hughes, *Post-Industrial America*, p. 10.

Chapter 2

1. Adna Ferrin Weber, *The Growth of the Cities in the Nineteenth Century* (Ithaca, N.Y.: Cornell University Press, 1899).

2. Peter Morrison, "Population Movements and the Shape of Urban Growth: Implications for Public Policy," in *Population, Distribution and Policy*, ed. Sarah Mills Mazie (Washington: U.S. Government Printing Office, 1972), pp. 290-296.

3. Henry S. Shryock and Charles Nam, "Education Selectivity of Inter-Regional Migration," *Social Forces* 43, no. 3 (1965):299-310.

4. Bureau of Census, "Current Population Survey of October 1946," in *Population, Distribution and Policy*, ed. Sarah Mills Mazie.

5. John B. Lansing and Eva Mueller, *The Geographic Mobility of Labor* (Ann Arbor: Survey Research Center, Institute for Social Research, 1967), p. 38.

6. Saben, "Geographic Mobility and Employment Status," *Monthly Labor Review* 87(August 1964):876, table 5.

7. Lansing and Mueller, *Geographic Mobility of Labor*, p. 3.

8. Morrison, "Population Movements," pp. 290-296.

9. V.R. Fuchs, *Differentials in Hourly Earnings by Region and City Size, 1959* (New York: National Bureau of Economic Research, 1967).

10. Niles Hansen, *Location Preference, Migration and Regional Growth* (New York: Praeger, 1973), p. 32.

11. Harry K. Schwarzweller, "Migration and the Changing Rural Scene," *Rural Sociology* 44(1979):7.

12. Ibid., p. 10.

13. Curtis C. Roseman, "Changing Migration Patterns within the United States" (Washington, D.C.: Association of American Geographers, Resource Paper 77-2, 1977).

14. Calvin Beale, *The Revival of Population Growth in Non-Metropolitan America* (Washington: U.S. Department of Agriculture, Economic Research Service, 1975).

15. Louis Harris and Associates, Inc., *A Survey of Public Attitudes toward Urban Problems and toward the Impact of Scientific and Technical Developments, Study 2040, November 1970.*

16. Gallup Opinion Survey (Princeton: American Institute of Public Opinion, August 1975).

17. Sarah Mills Mazie, ed., *Population, Distribution and Policy*, p. 605.

18. Robert Marrins and John D. Wellman, "The Quality of Non-Metro-politan Living: Evaluations, Behavior, and Expectations of Northern Michigan Residents" (Ann Arbor: University of Michigan Survey Research Center, 1978), p. 263.

19. Lewis A. Ploch, "The Reversal in Migration Patterns—Some Rural Development Consequences," *Rural Sociology* 32, no. 2 (Summer 1978):294-303.

20. James J. Zuiches and Edwin J. Carpenter, "Residential Preferences and Rural Development Policy" (USDA paper prepared for Rural Development Perspectives, no. 1, September 1978).

21. George Sternlieb and James W. Hughes, "New Regional and Metro-politan Realities of America," *Journal of the American Institute of Planning* 43, no. 3 (July 1977):228.

22. George Sternlieb and James W. Hughes, *Post-Industrial America: Metropolitan Decline and Inter-Regional Job Shifts* (Center for Urban Policy Research, Rutgers University, 1975), p. 64.

23. George Sternlieb and James W. Huges, "New Regional and Metropolitan Realities," p. 230.

24. Bernard L. Weinstein, and Robert E. Firestine, *Regional Growth and Decline in the United States: The Rise of the Sun Belt and the Decline of the Northeast* (New York: Praeger, 1978), p. 19.

25. Ibid., p. 26.

26. Ibid.

27. Michael J. McManus, "The Frostbelt Fights" (Albany, N.Y.: Empire State Report, October-November 1976), p. 344.

28. U.S. Department of Commerce, Bureau of the Census, "Current Population Reports," Series P-25, no. 646 (February 1977), pp. 2 and 4.

29. David J. Morgan, "Patterns of Population Distribution: A Residential Preference Model and Its Dynamic" (Chicago: University of Chicago Press, 1978), p. 22.

30. John Wardwell, "Equilibrium and Change in Non-Metropolitan Growth," *Rural Sociology* 42, no. 2 (Summer 1977):156-179.

31. Alfred J. Brown, *The Framework of Regional Economics in the United Kingdom* (Cambridge, England: Cambridge University Press, 1972).

32. Larry Blackwood and Edwin Carpenter, "The Importance of Anti-Urbanism in Determining Residential Preference and Migration Patterns," *Rural Sociology* 43, no. 1 (1978):31-47.

Chapter 3

1. Jane Jacobs, *The Death and Lives of Great American Cities* (New York: Random House, 1961), p. 444.

2. John N. Jackson, *The Urban Future: A Choice between Alternatives* (London: George Allen Unwin Ltd., 1972), p. 326.

3. Jacobs, *Great American Cities*, p. 447.

4. Constantinos Apostolou Doxiodis, *Action for Human Settlements* (New York: W.W. Norton & Co., 1976).

5. René Dubos, "Man Adapting," in *Environment for Man*, ed. W. Ewald, Jr. (Bloomington, Ind.: Indiana University Press, 1967).

6. *Saturday Review*, 28 April 1979.

7. John J. Palen, *The Urban World* (New York: McGraw-Hill, 1975).

8. Dubos, "Man Adapting,"

9. Editors of *The Ecologist, A Blueprint for Survival* (Boston: Houghton Mifflin, 1972).

10. Dubos, "Man Adapting."

11. Scott Greer, *The Emerging City* (Glencoe, Ill.: Free Press, 1972), p. 205.

12. Charles Abrams, *The City Is a Frontier* (New York: Harper Colophon Books, 1976), p. 155.

Chapter 4

1. It is the intention of the author that the commission establish goals for balanced growth in an advisory capacity.

2. *Urban and Rural American: Policies for Future Growth* (Washington, D.C.: Advisory Commission on Intergovernmental Relations, 1968), p. 15.

3. James L. Sundquist, *Dispersing Population: What America Can Learn from Europe* (Washington, D.C.: Brookings Institution, 1975), p. 5.

4. Governors' Conference, *Proceedings of the National Governors' Conference*, annual meeting, 1968, pp. 135-137.

5. White House, National Goals Research Staff, "Toward Balanced Growth: Quantity with Quality" (July 1970), p. 45.

6. Donald Canty, ed. *The New City* (New York: Praeger, 1969).

7. Richard Nixon, "State of the Union Message," 22 January 1970.

8. Sundquist, *Dispersing Population*, p. 9.

9. U.S., Congress, Committee on Community Development, the Domestic Council, "Report on National Growth and Development," 1974.

10. Sarah Mills Mazie, and Steve Rawlings, "Public Attitudes toward Population Distribution Issues," in *Report of the Commission on Population Growth in the American Future* (Washington: U.S. Government Printing Office, 1972), p. 609.

11. Ibid.

12. Calvin Beale, *The Revival of Population Growth in Non-Metropolitan America* (Washington: U.S. Department of Agriculture, Economic Research Service, 1975).

13. E.F. Schumacher, *Small Is Beautiful* (New York: Harper and Row, 1973).

Chapter 5

1. Ebenezer Howard, *Garden Cities of Tomorrow* (1898; definitive ed., with editorial preface by F.J. Osborn and introductory essay by Lewis Mumford, Cambridge, Mass.: MIT Press, 1946).

2. Frederick J. Osborn, preface to *Garden Cities of Tomorrow*, by Ebenezer Howard, p. 18.

3. Edward Bellamy, *Looking Backward, 2000-1887* (1888; Cambridge, Mass.: Harvard University Press, 1967).

4. Frederick J. Osborn, preface to *Garden Cities* p. 21.

5. Howard, *Garden Cities.*

6. Frederick J. Osborn, *Green Belt Cities* (New York: Schocken Books, 1969), p. 169.

7. Lewis Mumford, introduction to *Green Belt Cities*, by Frederick J. Osborn, p. 2.

8. Frederick J. Osborn and Arnold Whittick, *The New Towns* (Cambridge, Mass.: MIT Press, 1963), p. 3.

9. Mumford, introduction to *Green Belt Cities*, p. 2.

10. Howard, *Garden Cities*, p. 61.

11. Osborn, *Green Belt Cities*, p. 2.

12. Robert Fishman, *Urban Utopians of the Twentieth Century* (New York: Basic Books, 1977) p. 14.

13. Osborn, *Green Belt Cities*, p. 172.

14. Howard, *Garden Cities*, p. 51.

15. Fishman, *Urban Utopians*, pp. 59-63.

16. *Fabian News*, December 1898, in F.J. Osborn's preface to *Garden Cities of Tomorrow*, p. 11.

17. Murray Bookchin, *The Limits of the City* (New York: Harper Colophon, 1974), p. 119.

18. E.A. Gutkind, *The Twilight of the Cities* (Glencoe, Ill.: Free Press, 1962), pp. 123-126.

19. Jane Jacobs, *The Death and Life of Great American Cities* (New York: Random House, 1961), p. 289.

Chapter 6

1. Frederick J. Osborn, *Green Belt Cities* (New York: Schocken Books, 1969), p. 56.

2. Lloyd Rodwin, *The British New Towns Policy* (Cambridge, Mass.: Harvard University Press, 1956), p. 18.

3. Marion Clawson and Peter Hall, *Planning and Urban Growth: An Anglo-American Comparison* (Baltimore: Johns Hopkins University Press, 1972), p. 39.

4. Hans Blumenfeld, *The Modern Metropolis: Its Origins, Growth, Characteristics and Planning* (Cambridge, Mass.: MIT Press, 1966), p. 67.

5. Pierre Merlen, *New Towns* (London: Methuen, 1971), p. 28.

6. Clawson and Hall, *Planning and Urban Growth*, p. 206.

7. *Town and Country Planning* 39, no. 1, 1971.

8. Clawson and Hall, *Planning and Urban Growth*, p. 205.

9. *New Communities: Problems and Potentials* (Washington: U.S. Department of Housing and Urban Development, New Communities Administration, December 1976), p. 12.

10. Testimony of David Hall, executive director of British Town and Country Planning Association, at "The Oversight Hearings on the New Community Program before the Subcommittee on Housing and Community Development of House Committee on Banking, Currency and Housing," 1st sess., 1975, p. 333.

11. Morton White and Lucia White, *The Intellectual Versus the City* (Cambridge, Mass.: Harvard University Press, 1962), pp. 155-178.

12. Jane Addams, *Twenty Years At Hull House* (New York: Macmillan, 1910).

13. John Dewey, *Public and Its Problems* (New York: H. Holt and Co. 1927).

14. Ibid., p. 216.

15. Clarence Stein, *Toward New Towns for America* (Cambridge, Mass., MIT Press, 1956), p. 14.

16. Ibid., p. 15.

17. Joseph Arnold, *The New Deal in the Suburbs: History of Greenbelt Town Program 1935-1954* (Columbus: Ohio State University Press, 1971), p. 16.

18. Ibid., pp. 15-16.

19. Edward P. Eichler, "Why New Communities," in *New Towns and the Suburban Dream*, ed. Irving Lewis Allan (New York: Kennikat Press, 1977).

20. Gurney Breckenfeld *Columbia and the New Towns* (New York: Ives Washburn, 1971), p. 119.

21. *New Communities*.

22. *Hearings on sec. 1354 before Subcommittee on the Senate Committee on Banking and Currency*, 89th Cong., 1st sess., 1965, p. 329.

23. Donald Canty, ed., *The New City* (New York: Praeger, 1969).

24. *New Communities*, Appendix D, "Achievements and Potentials," pp. 5-8.

25. Ibid., p. 9.

26. *New Communities*, Appendix C, "An Assessment of the Causes of Current Problems," by Booz, Allen and Hamilton, Inc., p. 89.

27. Ibid., p. 78.

28. Ibid., p. 79.

29. Ibid., pp. 80-83.

30. Ibid., p. 107.

31. Ibid., p. 4.

32. "Classic Fed Failure," *Multi-Housing News* (New York: Gralla Publishing Co.) December 1978.

33. *New Communities*, Appendix C., pp. 51-58.

34. Maurice Parkim, *City Planning in Soviet Russia* (Chicago: University of Chicago Press, 1973), p. 12.

35. Ibid.

36. David T. Catrell, "Soviet Cities and Consumer Welfare Planning," in *The City in Russian History*, ed. Michael F. Hamm (Lexington, Ky.: University of Kentucky Press, 1976), p. 257.

37. Ibid.

38. Ibid., p. 271.

39. Parkim, *City Planning*, p. 31.

40. William Taubman, *Governing Soviet Cities* (New York: Praeger, 1973).

Chapter 7

1. Lewis Mumford, *The Urban Prospect* (New York: Harcourt, Brace and World, 1968), p. 18.

2. Morton White, and Lucia White, *The Intellectual versus the City* (Cambridge, Mass.: Harvard University Press, 1962), p. 14.

3. Frank Wright, *The Future of Architecture* (New York: Horizon Press, 1953), pp. 165-175.

4. Ibid.

5. Robert C. Twombley, *Frank Lloyd Wright* (New York: Harper and Row, 1973), p. 177.

6. Mumford, *Urban Prospect*, p. 130.

7. Victor Gruen, *The Heart of Our Cities* (New York: Simon and Schuster, 1964), pp. 266-296.

8. Mitchell Gordon, *Sick Cities* (Baltimore: Pengiun Books, 1963), p. 416.

9. E.A. Gutkind, *The Twilight of the Cities* (Glencoe, Ill.: Free Press, 1962), pp. 151-194.

10. Ibid., p. 161.

11. Murray Bookchin, *The Limits of the City* (New York: Harper Colophon, 1972); see also Paul Goodman, *Communities* (Chicago: University of Chicago Press, 1947).

12. Editors of *The Ecologist, A Blueprint for Survival* (Boston: Houghton Mifflin, 1972).

13. Bookchin, *Limits of the City*, pp. 2-3.

14. William H. Whyte, *The Last Landscape* (Garden City, N.Y.: Doubleday, 1968), pp. 333-335.

15. John Eli Burchard, "The Limitations of Utilitarianism as a Basis for Determining Joy," in *Man and the Modern City*, ed. Elizabeth Geen (Pittsburgh: University of Pittsburgh Press, 1963), pp. 18-24.

16. Otis Dudley Duncan, "Optimum Size of City," in *Reader in Urban Sociology*, ed. Paul Hatt and Albert Reiss (Glencoe, Ill.: Free Press, 1951), p. 381.

17. Ibid.

Chapter 8

1. Adam Smith, *The Wealth of Nations*, bk. 3, chap. 3 1776.

2. Murray Bookchin, *The Limits of the City* (New York: Harper Colophon, 1974), p. 26.

3. John J. Palen, *The Urban World* (New York: McGraw-Hill, 1975), p. 21.

4. Ibid., p. 28.

5. Arnold Toynbee, *Cities on the Move* (Oxford, England: Oxford University Press, 1970), p. 19.

6. Leonard Reisman, *The Urban Process and New Theory of City* (Glencoe, Ill.: Free Press, 1964), p. 151.

7. Sam Bass Warner, Jr., *The Private City* (Philadelphia: University of Pennsylvania Press, 1968), p. 3.

8. J. Franklin Jameson, *The American Revolution Considered as a Social Movement* (Princeton: Princeton University Press, 1930).

9. Paul W. Gates, *History of Public Land Law Development* (Washington, D.C.: U.S. Government Printing Office, 1968), pp. 33-48.

10. Sam Bass Warner, Jr., *The Urban Wilderness* (New York: Harper and Row, 1972), p. 18.

11. Blake McKelvey, *American Urbanization: A Comparative History* (Glenview, Ill.: Scott Foresman & Co., 1973), p. 65.

12. Bernard Rudolfsky, *Streets for People* (New York: Doubleday, 1969), p. 110.

13. Ibid., p. 52.

14. Bayrd Still, *Urban America: A History with Documents* (Boston: Little Brown & Co., 1974), p. 68.

15. McKelvey, *American Urbanization*, p. 27.

16. Warner, *Urban Wilderness*, p. 84.

17. Charles Glaab, *History of Urban America* (New York: Macmillan, 1967), pp. 154-155.

18. Sam Bass Warner, Jr., *Street Car Suburbs* (Washington, D.C.: Howard University Press, 1962), p. 2.

19. Ibid., p. 3.

20. Anthony Downs, *Opening Up the Suburbs: An Urban Strategy for America* (New Haven, Conn.: Yale University Press, 1973), pp. 60-65.

21. Warner, *Street Car Suburbs*, p. 9.

22. Robert Ezra Park, *Human Communities: The City in Human Ecology* (Glencoe, Ill.: Free Press, 1952).

23. Frederick Howe, *The City: The Hope for Democracy* (Seattle: University of Washington Press, 1906).

24. Morton White and Lucia White, *The Intellectual versus the City* (Cambridge, Mass.: Harvard University Press, 1962).

25. Leo Marx, *The Machine in the Garden* (Oxford, England: Oxford University Press, 1964).

26. Frederick C. Howe, "The City as a Socializing Agency," *Journal of Sociology* (March 1912):590.

Chapter 9

1. John J. Palen, *The Urban World* (New York: McGraw-Hill, 1975), p. 47.

2. Ibid., p. 49.

3. John Ottensman, *The Changing Spatial Structure of American Cities* (Lexington, Mass.: Lexington Books, 1975), p. 14.

4. Bernard L. Weinstein, and Robert E. Firestine, *Regional Growth and Decline in the United States: The Rise of the Sun Belt and the Decline of the Northeast* (New York: Praeger, 1978), p. 45.

5. John H. Mollenhopf, "The Crisis of the Public Sector in American Cities," in *Fiscal Crisis of American Cities*, ed. Roger E. Alcaly (New York: Vintage Books, 1977), p. 116.

6. C.B. Sparr, *Distribution of Wealth in the United States*, 1896.

7. Charles Tilly, "Race and Migration to the American City," in *Metropolitan Enigma*, ed. James Q. Wilson (New York: Anchor Books, 1970), p. 143.

8. Ibid., p. 153.

9. Sarah Mills Mazie, *Population, Distribution and Policy* (Washington: U.S. Government Printing Office, 1972) p. 240.

10. Ibid.

11. Tilly, "Race and Migration," p. 143.

12. Clyde V. Kiser, *Sea Island to City* (New York: Columbia University Press, 1932), p. 144.

13. C. Wright Mills, *The Puerto Ricans Journey: New York's Newest Migrants* (New York: Harper and Row, 1950), p. 45.

14. Hope T. Eldridge and Dorothy Swaine Thomas, *Population Redistribution and Economic Growth, United States, 1870-1950* (Philadelphia: American Philosophical Society, 1964), 3:368.

15. Palen, *Urban World*, p. 47.

16. Paul F. Cressy, "Population Succession in Chicago, 1898-1930," *American Journal of Sociology* 44(1938):59.

Chapter 10

1. Sarah Mills Mazie, *Report of the Commission on Population Growth in the American Future* (Washington: U.S. Government Printing Office, 1972), p. 15.

2. Ray Marshall, "Manpower Policies and Rural America," *Manpower* (April 1972):15.

3. Niles Hansen, *Locational Preference Migration and Regional Growth: A Study of the South and Southwest United States* (New York: Praeger, 1973).

4. George Sternlieb and James W. Hughes, *Post-Industrial America, Metropolitan Decline and Inter-Regional Job Shifts* (New Brunswick, N.J.: Rutgers University, 1975), p. 9.

5. Sam Bass Warner, Jr., *The Urban Wilderness* (New York: Harper and Row, 1972), p. 44.

6. Constance McLaughlin Green, *The Rise of Urban America* (New York: Harper and Row, 1965), p. 149.

7. Charles N. Glaab and A. Theodore Brown, *A History of Urban America* (New York: Macmillan, 1967), p. 278.

8. Clay Grady, *Close Up: How to Read the American City* (New York: Praeger, 1973), p. 177.

9. York Wilbern, *The Withering Away of the City* (University: University of Alabama Press, 1964), p. 14.

10. Mitchell Gordon, *Sick Cities* (Baltimore: Penquin Books, 1963), p. 18.

11. Peter Wolf, *The Future of the City* (New York: Whitney Publishers, 1974), p. 64.

12. Lewis Mumford, *The City in History* (New York: Harcourt, Brace and World, 1961.

13. Hans Blumenfeld, *The Modern Metropolis: Its Origins, Characteristics and Planning* (Cambridge, Mass.: MIT Press, 1966).

14. Alfred Cobban, *Rousseau and the Modern State* (London: Allen and Unwin, 1934).

15. Robert Dahl, "The City and the Future of America," in *Political Power, and the Urban Crisis* ed. Alan Shank (Boston: Holbrook Press 1969).

16. Charles Tilly, *Race and Migration to the American City*, in *Metropolitan Enigma*, ed. James Q. Wilson (New York: Anchor Books, 1970), p. 144.

17. Don Martindale, introduction to *The City*, by Max Weber (Glencoe, Ill.: Free Press, 1962).

18. Sarah Mills Mazie, ed., *Population Distribution and Policy* (Washington: U.S. Government Printing Office, 1972), p. 605.

Chapter 11

1. *House Magazine* (New York: McGraw Hill Publications, July 1979), p. 9.

2. *New York Magazine*, July 1979.

3. Anthony Downs, *Opening Up the Suburbs: An Urban Strategy for America* (New Haven, Conn.: Yale University Press, 1973), p. 5.

4. *Saturday Review*, 28 April 1979.

Chapter 12

1. Oliver C. Winston, "Urbanization Pattern for the United States," editorial, *Washington Post*, 10 October 1967.

2. Richard D. Lamm, "Local Growth: Focus of a Changing American Value Equilibrium," vol. 1, no. 1, January 1973.

3. Harry Richardson, *The Economics of Urban Size* (Lexington, Mass.: Lexington Books, D.C. Heath, 1973).

4. Luther Tweeten and Yau Chi Lu, "Attitudes as a Measure of Optimal Place of Residence," *Social Science Journal* 13, no. 2 (April 1976).

5. Ibid.

6. Gurney Breckenfeld, *Columbia and the New Towns* (New York: Ives Washburn, 1971), pp. 175-176.

7. Jane Jacobs, *The Death and Life of Great American Cities* (New York: Random House, 1961).

Index

About the Author

John Oosterbaan received the B.A. from the University of Michigan, and the J.D. from Northwestern University Law School. He is senior partner in the law firm of Oosterbaan, York and Cooper in Kalamazoo, Michigan, and chairman of the board of American Homestead Corporation, a real-estate investment organization affiliated with Connecticut Mutual Life Insurance Company.

Mr. Oosterbaan was the vice mayor of Kalamazoo from 1971 to 1973 and served on the City Commission from 1969 to 1971. He is the founder and president of the Society of Population Dispersal, Inc., an organization providing information on the benefits of population dispersal. Mr. Oosterbaan has visited new towns in Great Britain, France, and the USSR.